HENLEY-IN-ARI

LIFE FROM THE P

CW00959687

Dedicated to my wife Irene

HENLEY-IN-ARDEN

LIFE FROM THE PAST

By

R. Charles Welham

BREWIN BOOKS

First published
by Brewin Books, Studley, Warwickshire, B80 7LG
in May 1993

ISBN 1 85858 018 8

British Library Cataloguing in Publication Data.
A Catalogue record for this book is available from the British Library

Typeset by Avon Dataset, Bidford on Avon, Warwickshire, B50 4JH
Printed and bound at The Alden Press, Oxford

Contents

Acknowledgements

Most of the historical information I have quoted has been taken from William Cooper's book *Henley-in-Arden*. I record my sincere acknowledgement for this help.

I also acknowledge with gratitude my thanks to Bernard O'Donnell for making so many of the photographs used in this book available to me from his personal collection, without which I think this book would have been less interesting.

Foreword

My wife and I came to Henley-in-Arden in January 1964. I retired from business in 1975.

During this period I became acquainted with quite a number of the residents, — many had been born here. I often heard stories about the past and used to think to myself that when these people died so would their experiences.

Sometime during 1977 I made up my mind to go and see Mr. Beck Harris, one of our local butchers at that time, and ask him if he would be good enough to tell me of some of his earliest recollections. He was most kind and readily agreed. I spent five or six afternoons with him, scribbling down on my pad as hard as I coud without missing anything he was saying. I had no mechanical devices with me to record what I was being told.

At the end of my meetings with Mr. Harris I decided that I would approach other people who I knew would have been born about the turn of this century and ask them if they would mind telling me about their memories. Here again I was received with the same kindness that had been shown to me by Mr. Harris.

I need hardly say that with all of us, memories are better with some than with others, especially bearing in mind the ages of those good people I had the pleasure of listening to.

It was not until 1986 that I began to wonder whether or not my writings would have any appeal. In this connection I am grateful to Mr. Chris Lane, Chairman of T.M.I. (Henley-in-Arden) and his secretary Mrs Cindy Price, for their help and encouragement to proceed further.

It was then suggested to me that it might be worthwhile to include details of some of the history of Henley-in-Arden. Whilst this suggestion appealed I thought I could be getting out of my depth, but the advice was to 'use my own words and keep it brief'.

It took me quite a time to make a start on the historical section and I hope that you, the reader, will bear with me because this has been put together using 'my own words'.

I would say that I have admired so much the people I have talked to because many of them knew what it was like to be a member of a poor family, yet this never seemed to prevent them from enjoying some measure of happiness from their lives. No one I spoke to regretted being born when they were. A spirit prevailed then which unfortunately now appears to have disappeared.

I have also been struck by the kindness of many who were better off towards those less well off.

I should have liked to have had the time to visit more people but I was uncertain as to what would happen, if anything, to my writings. In this connection I am grateful to Alan Brewin of Brewin Books, Studley, for all his help in editing and publishing all I have written. I appreciate that many of the experiences quoted by those people I have talked to would have been shared by others in rural communities.

In conclusion and on a more personal note, I do think that most of us have a great deal more to be thankful for when we compare what we have with what was available to the people I have talked to when they were young. I do understand that like a lot of things in life, it's a compromise.

Henley-in-Arden

Henley-in-Arden is situated eight miles north of Stratford-upon-Avon and 14 miles south of Birmingham. To London the distance is 102 miles. This information is given on a stone slab at the base of the wall fronting milestone cottage, 185 High Street. This slab is thought to have been erected by the Turnpike Trust, a body set up to adminster the various turnpikes and maintenance of roads, towards the end of the 18th century. One of the statutory laws governing this trust was that milestones should be placed at appropriate distances along the highway as helpful information to all users. The main street is reckoned to be a mile long measured from the Golden Cross Hotel to the end of the white railings at the Buckley Green turn.

Henley-in-Arden is not mentioned in the Domesday survey: the lands which now form this town would have been included with those of Wootton Wawen. There are two parishes, Beaudesert and Henley-in-Arden, the former being the older but for most administrative purposes the two parishes are combined to form the town of Henley-in-Arden.

In years gone by a brook ran down the east side of the main street from the mill at the north end, past the market cross down Back Lane then channelled under St. Johns Church. It would then have re-entered the River Alne between the church and the Warwick Road. The River Alne rises some four or five miles to the north of Henley and reaches the town on the eastern outskirts. It is now a very pleasant backwater running parallel to the High Street which can be walked by footpath. The river flows south-west to Wootton Wawen and then on to Alcester where it joins the River Arrow. In the past the Alne was undoubtedly a much larger river which supplied water power to the mills at Henley and Blackford.

The Mount. Today it serves as a recreational area (although privately owned) for the people of Henley and many others beside. It can be reached by going to the end of Beaudesert Lane which leads off the High Street by St. Johns Church. From the top of the Mount there are splendid views over most of Beaudesert and Henley-in-Arden. This was the site for Beaudesert Castle, the home of the De-Montforts. It is not difficult to trace the outline of where the castle once stood. It is most likely to have been constructed of timber and local stone. Unfortunately there are no illustrations available as to what the castle looked like. In a survey of Warwickshire carried out in the 16th century there is no mention of a Beaudesert Castle so it must be assumed that the building had fallen into ruins, because it is known that sometime during the 14th century, because of default of heirs, the De-Montforts lands passed to the Earl of Warwick. The ancestors of both of these families had been associates of William the Conqueror.

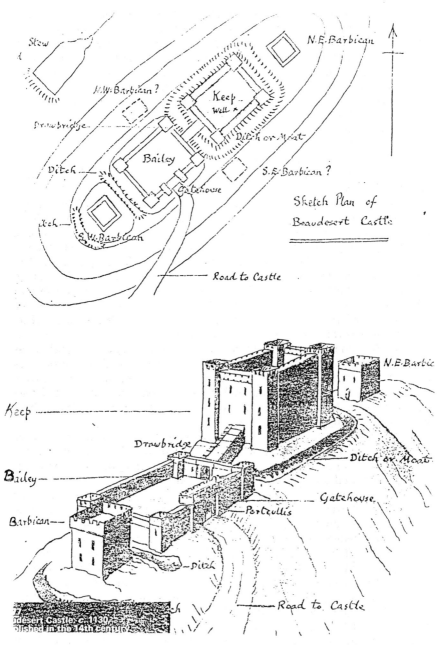

An artists impression of what Beaudesert Castle may have looked like.

Towards the end of the 12th century Thurstan De-Montfort built his castle and within a short period of time was granted permission to hold a market and fair each week within the walls of the castle. Even in those days it could be dangerous for traders and others not to have some form of protection from robbers and the like. The market as now would have been an attraction to traders and shoppers, Henley undoubtedly owes its existance to the De-Montforts who settled in this place. Timber for building purposes was unlikely to have been too much of a problem.

In 1265 at the battle of Evesham, the head of the De-Montforts at that time, Peter, was killed fighting against the king, Henry III. Shortly afterwards the settlement which had been built up around the castle, was burnt down. It is not known for certain whether this was through accident or out of revenge that the Lord of the Manor, Peter De-Montfort, had taken up arms against the king. It is apparent that the settlement did recover to establish itself, for in 1449 Sir Ralph Boteler, then Lord of the Manor, obtained for Henley-in-Arden a most important charter, confirming previous privileges and concessions with more added. This charter together with its seal granted by Henry VI. hangs in the Guildhall (upstairs). The granting of rights to hold a market provided useful sources of revenue to the Lords of the Manor through duties and taxes levied on sales of animals and other merchandise. There would also have been opportunities for people other than traders to earn money from the activities created by the market. In other words the beginnings of a 'Market Economy?'

From this time onwards the town has grown gradually and its position as a trading centre and place of work is borne out by the number of properties that can trace their origins back to the 16th and 17th centuries. Some were possibly built from stones and timber taken from the old castle. Some cottages which have been demolished in the past have revealed timbers which had already been used once.

In the 19th century Henley was still somewhat isolated, although coaches used the main road running through Henley on their way to Stratford-upon-Avon, Oxford and London. It was not until the coming of the railway that the town showed a marked increase in its population.

The first railway line was started in 1861 by a private company. The starting point was at the north end of the high street where Abrasive Developments now have their offices and works. The line climbed steadily away from Henley until it passed under Edge Lane and through the first cutting when it began to level out. Within a few years work had to stop through lack of funds and it was not until the 1890s that the Great Western Railway took over the project which was finally completed and the line opened for traffic in 1895. This line from Henley joined the main G.W.Rly. line to Birmingham and Leamington Spa at Kingswood, a junction south of Lapworth. There is a story that one engine driver bringing a train from Birmingham and not being too familiar with the line and its gradient down to Henley was unable to stop the train at the station and ploughed on through the stop blocks, the train coming to rest just before reaching the brook. The original engine shed is still standing, possibly used for storage. This line had a very limited life, closing in 1915. This was undoubtedly due to the opening of the North Warwickshire Line in 1908 which was also operated by the G.W.Rly. There was a more frequent service to Birmingham than with the original line plus the advantage of a more direct link with Stratford-upon-Avon, which would have appealed to the people of Henley. This line also connected with lines to the West Country and it was not long before the Railway began to run excursions to Weston-Super-Mare and Weymouth. There were bound to be other places which would have given many people their first opportunity to see the sea.

This line also suffered an accident in its early days. In 1911 a train from Birmingham, not scheduled to stop at Henley, was by accident switched into the sidings to the west of the station and came to rest on its side.

De-railment at Henley Station midnight 24/25 June, 1911 when a Snow Hill to Bristol train chartered by a Bristol Bowls club was switched by mistake into the sidings. Driver and Fireman scolded, nine passengers injured.

Henley Gas Company. The first meeting was held in 1862 when a very enthusiastic civil engineer outlined details of the costs involved for erecting a power house and laying of pipes. He went so far as to estimate the return shareholders could expect on their investment. Henley got their gas works which was situated at the end of

Alne Close, but it would appear that there was very little return for the share-holders, Solihull Gas eventually took over the supply of gas to Henley about 1950.

Henley Water Supply. In the middle of the last century most people relied on wells for their water requirements. Towards the end of the century and into the present one small reservoirs were built and pipes laid to various villages including Henley. This system of supply lasted until the late 30s when an agreement was reached with the City of Birmingham for them to supply water by extending their mains from Hockley Heath. Today the Severn Trent water Authority are responsible for supplies.

Electricity. This came to Henley at the commencement of the 30s.

Development

The population at the turn of the century was just over a thousand souls, this total had not changed very much during the past fifty years. The layout of the town was almost the same as it had always been, the main street and a single side turning, Beaudesert Lane. At the southern end of the main street there was a road which ran across connecting Warwick through Henley to Redditch.

The houses and cottages on these thoroughfares had remained unchanged for a hundred years or more and in quite a number of cases twice this length of time. Most of the cottages would have been rented.

In 1908 Station Road was opened up to give access to the new station on the North Warwickshire line.

Since this time there began a trickle of families mainly from the Birmingham area who came to live in Henley. This has gained momentum since the start of the second World War largely because of the development that has taken place within the town and the increase in the number of family cars.

Round about the time of the first World War a small number of houses were built privately along New Road, as a result of the previous lane being made more suitable for the increase in traffic using this bye way to Redditch and beyond. Barley Close, a cul-de-sac leading off New Road, was also a private development built around the same time.

In 1926 the Stratford Rural District Council was responsible for the commencement of the Cherry Orchard Estate to the west of the northern end of the High Street, a development the like of which Henley had not seen before. There would no doubt have been keen competition to acquire one of these properties which were reasonably spacious and, what would have been a real boon, with inside plumbing, which few cottages would have had. In addition each house had almost a miniature allotment at the rear and a pleasant garden in the front.

In about 1927 another small private development was started nearby which is the present Rose Avenue (cul-de-sac).

In 1929 a scaled down development similar to Cherry Orchard was started in School Road which must have been a welcome addition to the accommodation available to the people of the town.

During the second World War councillors were wrestling with the problems as to whether the land to the east of the southern end of the High Street was suitable and could be developed for housing. Finally it was decided to go ahead on this area which we know as 'The Pastures'. It consists of private dwellings as well as housing belonging to the District Council.

In 1962 the town witnessed the commencement of a major private development at Brook End. This was on land between housing on the west side of the High Street and the Birmingham-Stratford railway line. Since this time there has been practically continuous development of various sizes within the towns' boundary. The population now stands at almost 4000.

Henley in Arden pudding. Take ½ lb of the Flour
3 oz. dripping, 4 oz. sugar
1 Egg and a pinch of salt.
Mix with milk to a thick batter
grease basin, put jam at
bottom and steam for 2 hours.

Origin unknown.

Henley-in-Arden Churches

St. John's Church

Was built around the middle of the 15th century to replace a Chapel which was built about 1367 A.D. It is possible to verify this earlier date from the Worcester Diocesan records which confirm the Bishops authority to the townspeople of Henley, that at their own expense they were authorised to build a chapel. This authority was necessary because Henley parish was subject to the Church at Wootton Wawen. The parishioners made their request on the grounds of the distance they had to travel between Henley and Wootton in all weathers. Flooding of the River Alne and its tributaries presented a major problem because there is no mention of any bridges at this time. In the summer months there was always the risk of being waylaid by highway men.

List of Incumbents since 1745

Thomas Hall 1745.	Francis Dalrymple Lane 1915.
Richard Bird 1772.	Theodore John Cartwright 1921.
William Windsor Fitz-Thomas 1776.	William James Easterbrook 1930.
John Southall 1780.	Albert Henry Webb. 1946.
Poyntz Steward Ward. 1806.	Walter Edward Smith. 1967.
Thomas W. Jones. 1842.	Peter Hugh Bennett. 1975.
George Edward Bell. 1876.	John F. Ganjavi. 1989.

In 1847 new pews were installed which were square and high sided and it has been said that they resembled horse boxes. These would be rented to the leading parishioners. People too poor to pay for their seats were huddled together at the back or required to go up into the gallery which stretched across the west end of the nave and aisle. Over the altar against the east wall was another gallery which amongst other things contained the organ. Access to this gallery was from the Rector's vestry. There was also a three decker pulpit for parson and clerk. It is believed that the galleries and pews were cleared away in a major restoration carried out in 1856 at a cost of £900. An early post card photograph shows the present pulpit adjacent to the south wall in line with its present position.

The East Window is dedicated to the memory of H. Hopkins by his son, dated 1879 A.D.

The West Window is in memory of John and Sarah Cooke by their children dated 1882 A.D.

On the back of this post-card is written "New Organ. Pulpit moved to centre".

On the back of this photograph is written "Old Organ and Vestry Curtain" (Now in Ullenhall Church) Pulpit in original position. (Right hand side against south wall).

Within the entrance porch of St. Johns Church are two small glass windows dedicated to the memory of the Rev. G. Bell by his children dated 1924.

In 1881: AD The incumbent Rev. G. E. Bell caused quite a stir by having the choir robed in cassocks and surplices. For this action one of the things said about him was that he was a Papist. Some members of the church showed their displeasure by staying away from his services but he appears to have been a well respected person in that he remained in charge for more than another thirty years. In keeping with most churches the choir remains robed.

In 1900 A.D. Further renovations were carried out at a cost of £1,100 which was still insufficient to deal with the tower which required attention but had to wait until 1912. Up to this time the embattled tower had pinnacles at each corner in common with many other churches in Warwickshire but they had become unsafe and were taken down and never replaced. It would appear that there were insufficient funds to allow this work to be carried out.

In 1868 A.D. In this year the old clock which played tunes every three hours was replaced with the present clock which was made in Warwick by Alexander Sadler Simmons who was originally from Henley. The cost of £250 was raised by public subscription.

There are six bells, and originally there were seven but one small bell was removed to the Market House, close to the Market Cross, part of which was used as a free school.

In 1910 A.D. there was a commemoration service held in the belfry following the rehanging of the bells at a cost of £100. Today, 1990, an appeal has been launched for the rehanging of these same bells. The estimated cost for this work was £30,000. (Work completed in 1991).

In 1931 A.D. on Easter Day, a dedication and a memorial service was held to mark the introduction of electric lighting to the Glory of God and in memory of Theodore John Cartwright M. A. Oxon. Priest, Cannon of Coventry, Rector of Beaudesert-cum-Henley-in-Arden, 1921-1930.

The present organ is largely the results of the drive and enthusiasm of present day organist and choirmaster Geoffrey Gibbons LI.B. who has occupied this position since 1960. An appeal was launched in 1969 to replace the organ and within eighteen months the sum of £9,000 had been raised which was sufficient to ask J. W. Walker & Sons, of Ruislip, Middlesex, to build and install the present organ. A dedication service was held in St. Johns in December 1971 attended by The Very Rev. Cuthbert Bardsley D. D. Bishop of Coventry.

In 1976 A.D. an appeal was launched under the new incumbent Rev. Peter Bennett amounting to £57,000 for restoration work on both St. Johns and St. Nicholas Churches. The work was finally completed in 1986 at a total cost of almost £130,000. A considerable sum came from the Ministry of the Environment. For this, great credit must go to the late W. N. Hawkes. Hon. Architect, who supervised the work carried out by stone masons, Webb & Son. Worcester, and as a result of his close liaison with the Ministry enabled the Churches to receive maximum grants.

St. Johns Church — Henley-in-Arden

A brass tablet fixed to the north wall bears the following inscription.

> The names of those who in these years
> of war went forth from this place for
> God and the right and came not back
> are here inscribed to be honoured for
> evermore.

Holly Tree, close to the porch, replaced a yew tree at the turn of the century.

Roll of Honour

Harold Richard Arnold	Pte. Coldstream Guards	Killed 6th July, 1915.
Edward Hopkins	Pte. 9th R.Wk.Regt	Died of Wounds 8th October, 1915.
William Collins	Cpl. 1st R.Wk.Regt	Killed in action 11th October, 1916.
Francis Henry Woodward	Pte. 3rd R.Wk.Regt	Killed 11th Jan, 1917.
Frederick Charles Atkins	Sapper, R. E.	Killed 14th Jan, 1917.
Maurice Edward Horsnett	Pte. Hampshire Regt	Died in Hospital 8th April, 1917.
George Edward Andrews	Pte. 11th R. Wk.Regt	Killed 28th April, 1917.
William Louis Clare	Pte. R. Inniskilling Fus.	Missing believed killed 19th May, 1917.
William Sutton Findon	Pte. Canadian Expeditionary Force	Died of wounds 3rd July, 1917.

Lawrence John Arden Hodges	A.B. H.M.S. Vala.	Killed at Sea 21st August, 1917.
Harry Hugh Holt	Driver R.F.A.	Killed in Action 10th September, 1917.
Sidney Bickley	Pte. R. Dorset Regt	Killed in action 23rd March, 1918.
Thomas Sadler	Pte. 1st R.Wk.Regt	Died of wounds 4th April, 1918.
Owen Holt	Driver R.F.A.	Died of wounds 11th April, 1918.
George Amos Spears	Pte. 5th Dorset Regt	Killed in Action 12th April, 1918.
Albert Alfred Sammons	Pte. London Regt	Missing believed killed 25th April, 1918.
Arden Cotterell Coldicott M.C. Capt	15th R.Wk.Regt	Died of wounds in Germany. 4th August, 1918.
John Aubrey Hawkes. 2nd Lt.	Leicester Regt	Died of wounds 11th September, 1918.
Stephen Hastings	Pte. R.A.S.C.	Died at Havre 8th November, 1918.
Alfred Richards	A.B. R.N.	Killed in Action 23rd November, 1939.
Arthur Lowe.	Fireman N.F.S.	Killed by Enemy Action 14th November, 1940.
Joseph John Cave	Signalman. R. Signals.	Died on Active Service 30th April, 1941.
William Frederick Smith	Cpl. R.A.F.	Killed at sea 4th July, 1941.
Wilfred Norman Hattemore	Sgt. R.A.F.	Killed on active service 13th December, 1941.
Kenneth Bernard Wright. Flt. Lt.	R.A.F.	Missing believed killed 25 June, 1942.
Peter John Maxwell	Flt. Sgt. R.A.F. V.R.	Killed in action 19/ 20 September, 1942.
Albert Thomas Ritchings	Gunner. R.E.	Died at sea 1/2 October, 1942.
Albert Frederick Holmes	Cpl. R. Tank Regt.	Killed in action 21st February, 1943.
John Henry Warren	Driver R.A.S.C.	Died on active service 10th June, 1943.

Samuel Francis Padbury	Gnr. Scottish Horse	Died of wounds 18th February, 1944.
William Hobbins	Pte. R.M. CDO.	Killed in action 7th June, 1944.
Brian Richard Frederick Woodward	Tpr. R.A.C.	Killed in action 26th July, 1944.
Claude Avery Gilks	Pte. S. Staffords	Killed in action 8th August, 1944.
Norman Frederick Parkes	Sgt. S.A.P.C.	Died on active service 8th January, 1945.
Peter Thomas Newcombe	Lt. R.N.	Died on active service 8th February, 1945.

St. Nicholas Church

It is almost certain that this was the church built by the De-Montforts in the latter half of the 12th century, about 1170 A.D. 'exact date not known.' During the 15th century a tower was added. It would appear that the north wall was rebuilt further inwards, originally it would have been the same distance outwards from the chancel arch as the south wall. The east window is reported to be one of the finest Norman windows in the county and appears never to have been restored.* The vaulted roofing in the chancel dates from 1865. Restoration work carried out at this time included laying a plain stone floor and it is more than likely that a gallery at the west end would have been removed at this time. There are three bells in the tower. A certain amount of restoration was carried out to the stonework of the tower during 1930.

The adjacent rectory house, now a private dwelling, was built in 1868. A new rectory has just been built behind the church hall and slightly to the north.

Methodist Church

Records show that the earliest beginnings were round about the middle of the last century. Services began on a regular basis in an old building which was situated behind the present church which was built in 1894. There is a small gallery at the west end. Adjoining the church at the rear is a hall which has kitchen facilities which can be put to good use whenever the church requires to entertain its congregation and perhaps guests. The congregation is not large but every member gives their fullest support without which these buildings could not be maintained as they are.

*The East Window is to the memory of Wm. Welch Lea. died 1852.
The West Window is in memory of Margaret Ellen Elizabeth Lea. Died 1875.

Baptist Church, Henley-in-Arden after the fire of 1936.

Baptist Church

A congregation was first established as far back as 1688 in part of the premises immediately adjacent and to the north of the present church, called the Manse. A Chapel was built in 1822 — this building was subsequently replaced by another chapel in 1867 at a cost of £1700 which was the gift of Mr. G. F. Muntz of Umberslade. In 1936 a disastrous fire occurred which left only the walls standing. A new Church was built in 1937 which is the building we see today. In addition there is a most acceptable church hall at the rear. There is a stage and kitchen facilities.

St. Benedicts, Roman Catholic Church, Wootton Wawen.

The Roman Catholic Church

The church of Our Lady and St. Benedict is situated on the Alcester Road as it leaves Wootton Wawen. This Church was built in 1904. Previously services had been held in a chapel adjoining Wootton Hall which had been built at the beginning of the last century. Henley has two Parish Churches, St. Johns and St. Nicholas. A few years ago arrangements were made between The Parochial Church Council Beaudesert cum Henley-in-Arden, and the Roman Church, that the two Churches be used for worship each Sunday in the following way. From the beginning of October until the end of June, the Parish Church Congregation uses St. Johns and the Roman Catholics use St. Nicholas. Then from the beginning of July until the end of September the congregations switch over. The arrangements seem to work quite well.

Henley-in-Arden High Street

Henley Mill.
Although this building was erected towards the end of the last century records show that a mill has stood on this site for over eight hundred years.

Frederick Johnson Almshouses. 1904.
See notes on chemist.

Beechcroft.
Now a fairly modern housing development. Part of the frontage at the beginning of this century was occupied by a Mr. Badger, who was a baker and in addition sold groceries and sweets. He was noted for his infallable reply to his customers enquiry concerning his well being, which always brought forward the same 'pretty middling' comment.

Johnsons (Henley) Ltd.
Prior to the Johnson family setting up a carriers' business at this address round about 1920, the previous occupier went under the title of Frederick Richards & Co. Ltd. They had moved here from Camp Lane about 1880. Their main business was producing what they termed 'The Real Constitution Water'. In one of their adverts they showed two hands one holding a glass which contained the 'Constitution Water' which was according to other parts of the advert the remedy for so many ailments. In the other hand was the surgeon's knife. The choice was a matter for the reader. The business declined during the first World War and came to an end soon after. The business had commenced about 1810 so had lasted for over a hundred years. It would seem that the 'Water' had something to recommend it. The basis of the product was Lithiam Salt. When Johnsons bought the property it was known as Lithiam Place.

The Black Swan.
Has undoubtedly been associated with the social life of Henley for many years. At the turn of the century the Landlord was a Mr. Edkins — a name which has been associated with Henley and surrounding districts for quite a few centuries. His son Jack took over from his father.

Brook House.
47 High Street.
A benefactor from the 15th century gave this house to Henley for use as a school, but there are no records as to when it first served this purpose. It

The Black Swan, Landlord Ernest Edkins, 1910.

Brook House. Church of England Sunday School, 47 High Street.

would seem as if the property had a checkered career as a school, mainly through lack of funds. It ceased to operate as a school after the opening of the central school in 1884. It was used as an annexe to this school, boys being taught woodwork and girls domestic science. Part of the property was also used as a boys club and the Parish Church used the facilities on a Sunday for their school.

Ashbury House.
57 High Street.

A certain amount of fame is attached to this house because around the turn of the present century a Miss Annie Cooke lived here and was known for her beautiful garden and to a lesser extent her meanness. The author and playwright John Keble Bell son of the Rev. G. E. Bell, vicar of Henley (1876-1915) who wrote under the pen name of Keble Howard wrote a book 'The God in the Garden' with Miss Cooke as one of the central characters.

St. Loos.
77 High Street.

Originally three cottages. This was the first site that Mr. Fieldhouse C.B.E. J.P., newly appointed Lord of the Manor of Henley-in-Arden (1914), turned his attention to and eventually they became a single residence. At the beginning of the 30's the property became a successful restaurant under the management of Molly Green. It was called M.Gs. The second World War, which brought rationing of many foods, saw a decline in the business which closed shortly after the end of the war. The property has now reverted to a private residence.

46 High Street.
Brooklyn House.

This was the site of the British School, built in 1863 but closed when the central school opened in 1884.

The Blue Bell Inn.

Is 15th century. A very fine looking building since the plaster work was removed from the facing of the building to expose the timber framing. The high entrance leading to the rear was obviously designed for the stabling of horses and coaches which it undoubtedly catered for over very many years, not forgetting the passengers. It's hanging sign shows on one side a bluebell (flower) and on the other side a bell coloured blue.

Burman House.
50 High Street.

In the first instance this property was licenced as a mental asylum. The house will have taken its name from the person to whom the licence was granted (Mr. Thomas Burman) back in 1797. It remained in this capacity

The letters M. G. (Molly Green) can be seen on the left hand property (now St. Loos) which was a well known restaurant in the 1930s but did not survive after the second World War.

The Old Bell Inn before its facing timbers were exposed. The entrance to the Tan Yard can just be seen to the left of the two cottages.

M.G.'s

Aug. 16th

Meau

Molly Green

St. Loos.
Eods 305

Telephone : Henley-in-Arden 98.

From the Grill (40 mins.)

Mixed Grill	2/6	Sausage and Bacon	1/9
Rump Steak	1/9	Kidneys and Bacon	2/-
Fillet Steak	2/6	Liver and Bacon	2/-
Pocket Steak	2/6	Eggs and Bacon	1/9
Tournado of Steak	1/9	Ham and Eggs	2/3
Cutlets (2)	1/9	Ham or Bacon & Chips	1/6

Bacon and Tomatoes ... 1/6

Supper Dishes

2 Eggs on Chips	1/4	Spaghetti on Toast	1/-
2 Poached Eggs on Toast	1/3	Welsh Rarebit	1/-
		Mushrooms on Toast	1/6
Scrambled Eggs on Toast	1/3	Tomatoes on Toast	1/-
Eggs on Spinach	1/6	Soft Roes on Toast	1/3
Egg Hammy Topside	1/10	Sardines on Toast	1/-
Sweet Corn and Egg on Toast	1/6	Scotch Woodcock	1/3
		Stuffed Tomatoes	1/-
Buck Rarebit	1/3	Devils on Horseback	1/3
Heinz Beans on Toast	9d.	Sausage and Chips	1/4

Soups

Mushroom	6d.	Cream of Tomato	6d.
Asparagus	6d.	Julienne	6d.
Cream of Chicken	6d.	Kidney	6d.
Oxtail	6d.	Vegetable	6d.

Vegetables

Green Peas	6d.	Asparagus	1/-
Braised Celery	6d.	Boiled, Chipped, Saute	
Onions (fried)	6d.	or Mashed Potatoes	4d.
French Beans	6d.	Brussel Sprouts	4d.
Grilled Tomatoes	6d.	Cauliflower	4d.

Fish

Fillets of Plaice and Chips	1/6	Salmon Mayonnaise	2/3
Fried Sole and Chips	2/3	Lobster Mayonnaise	2/-
		Dressed Crab	1/9

Snack Bar

Hors-d'œuvres from	1/-	Sausages	1/-
Cold York Ham	1/6	Chicken	1/9 & 2/3
Ox Tongue	1/6	Steak & Kidney Pie	1/3
Roast Beef	1/6	Salads to order from	6d.
Salmon Mayonnaise	2/3	Devilled Egg Salad	1/3
Scotch Eggs	1/-	Pork Pie	6d.

Omelettes

M.G.'s Special	...	1/9
PLAIN OMELETTE	...	1/3
FINES HERBES „	...	1/6
SAVOURY „	...	1/6
FLORENTINE „	...	1/9
BACHELORS „	...	1/9
CHEESE „	...	1/6
HAM „	...	1/9
KIDNEY „	...	1/9
TOMATO „	...	1/6
SPANISH „	...	1/9
Chef's Special	...	1/9

SWEET OMELETTES :

PLAIN SWEET OMELETTE	...	1/-
JAM „	...	1/3
SURPRISE „	...	2/-
SOUFFLE „	...	1/9
RUM „	...	2/-

Sweets

Sherry Trifle	9d.	Jello Whip	6d.
Sweet Omelette	9d.	Fruit Tart	6d.
Fruit Salad and Cream	9d.	Whole Pears or	
Stem Ginger	9d.	Peaches	9d.
Kadota Figs	9d.	Blackcurrants & Cream	6d.
Jam Tart	4d.	Raspberries & Cream	9d.
Treacle Tart	4d.	Pineapple & Cream	6d.
Fruit Jellies	6d.		

Sundries and Beverages

Coffee	4d. and 6d.	Fresh Lemonade	4d.
Chocolate	6d.	Minerals	6d.
Bovril	6d.	Cheddar and	
Pot of Tea (Indian or China)	6d.	Cheshire Cheese	3d.
Ovaltine	6d.	Gorgonzola Cheese	4d.
Horlicks	6d.	Biscuits	2d.
Bournvita	6d.	Cream Ices	4d. & 6d.
Iced Coffee	6d.	Buttered Toast	4d.
Chocolate Biscuits, each	2d.	Fresh Thick Cream	3d.
Orange Juice	6d.	Pastries	2d.

Cigarettes

Afternoon Tea	...	1/3
Luncheon	2/- & 2/6	

Guests are invited to bring their own wines, or they can be obtained,
but must be paid for in all cases at the time the order is placed.
(Ask Waiter for Price List.)

N.B.—In Order to avoid disputes customers are
requested to examine the Bills presented by
the Waiters. Complaints should be lodged at
the Office.

Stephens.
Henley-in-Arden

(Sample of Menu).

The Police Station Henley-in-Arden. Built 1859. CNR. Station Rd. & High Street.

until 1882 when the patients were transferred to Glendossill (River House). At the turn of the century the house was used as a school. Round about 1930 the property was rented to Winn Riley's (post lady) mother, who offered accommodation as well as cafe facilities. Today all the accommodation plus extensions are fully utilised by Time Management International.

The Three Tuns Inn.
A 17th century Inn. Perhaps lacking in size, still plays a part in the social life of this town.

The Police Station.
Built in 1858 to provide accommodation for a police inspector plus three cells. A court house was built on in 1903 but was recently taken out of the Midland circuit.

The Gables.
105 High Street.
In 1448 at the instigation of the then Bishop of Worcester a hospital began to be built in Henley to the north of St. Johns Chapel. It is believed that this was the site. The building was more of an ecclesiastical than a medical institution designed for the relief of the poor and

Christmas time. 83 High Street.

travellers. John Hannett author and High Bailiff (1873-1893) lived for some years towards the end of his life in this house. It is recognised that speaking of a site to the north of St. Johns Chapel there could be a connection with the Guildhall.

Midland Bank.
68 High Street.
The present site was originally the old vicarage which consisted of two cottages which had been joined together. This property was once described as the prettiest house in Henley. The Rev. G. Bell and his family lived here for some twenty years from 1876. Midland Bank came to Henley in 1914 taking over the business of another firm of bankers. In those days they occupied the premises next door (66) before moving into their present offices at the end of the 60s.

The Kings Head.
70 High Street.
It is rather hard, looking at this property today, now a private residence, to think of it as a coaching inn with stabling at the rear. It has also been used for detaining persons overnight who were being marched from areas west of Henley to Warwick Goal. There could also have been persons detained and waiting to appear before the High Bailiff or magistrate. I

Now the premises of Westmacotts. Greengrocer. 95 High Street.

have been shown the large staples fixed into the skirting boards in the large front room which would have been used by people in chains.

The Bear Hotel.
84 High Street.
Originally The Bear and Ragged Staff. A 17th century building which is possibly confirmed by its present name 'Cromwell House'. It was used by our doctors as their surgery until November 1990, they have now moved to a purpose built surgery in Riverside. Cromwell House is now up for sale. The Bear closed down before the first World War but in 1903 they did run a very successful Quoits team having played seven matches and winning six. The quoits were iron rings.

Market Cross.
Dates from the 15th century. It was and still is a centre for all public activities and proclamations. Near by stood the market hall supported by wooden pillars which were taken down towards the end of the 18th century. Also close by were the stocks. One Richard Knight was on the 22nd October 1622 fined 3/4d. for wilfully breaking the town stocks during the night. In addition he was committed to sit in the stocks for one day.

The Old Vicarage originally two cottages. Once occupied by the Rev. G. E. Bell (1875-1914). Sometime after the first World War became the Old Vicarage cafe run by Mr. & Mrs. Walker. Now the site of the Midland Bank PLC (Mr Walker before his retirement was Head Master of the Council School).

Corner of Bear Lane and High St. Sometime before first World War.

The Market Cross with the George Inn in the background.

The celebration service following the signing of the Armistice on November 11th, 1918. In the background left 'The Old George' before its face lift. Next door is the small general shop run by the Miss Chetters, referred to by May Savage as providing so much pleasure to children before Christmas when they were allowed to walk round not only the shop but the living accommodation at the back which was opened up to display the seasonal gifts on offer. To the right the Stone House.

The Stone House, part of which was used as the Post Office and Telephone Exchange. Mr. Newcombe's petrol pumps flanking the market cross.

Taken outside the Post Office (Stone House). Date and occasion unknown.

The Mop during the early twenties.

H. Dorell, grocery & provisions, wines & spirits. Est. 1865. (Present site of Lloyds Bank PLC).

The present site of Lloyds Bank plc. when it was a garage about the year 1922. Mr. R. Newcombe had taken over the shop following extensive renovations carried out by Mr. W. J. Fieldhouse. It would seem that the R.A.C. thought it necessary to indicate which way the main road went. In 1933 a stone seat in memory of Dr. Ernest Nelson was placed against the railings protecting the market cross, facing up the street. As the result of a car running into the seat it was moved to its present site outside the porch of St. Johns Church.

On the left the Stone House (Post Office) next door Droitwich House where Frank Lowe at present Constable to the Court Leet was born.

Lloyds Bank.

This site at the commencement of the present century was a high class grocery and wine store owned by Mr. W. H. Dorrell. The property was acquired by Mr. W. J. Fieldhouse (Lord of the Manor) in about 1915. During repairs, plasterwork on the front was removed to expose the present vertical timbers. At the end of the first World War the property passed into the hands of Mr. Newcombe who used the shop for the sale and repairs of cycles. Within a short time the business had expanded to motor car repairs and the sale of petrol. Lloyds Bank purchased the property in 1943. They had previously occupied a part of the ground floor of the Guildhall where they had been since 1914.

The White Swan Hotel.

Is possibly one of the oldest building in Henley although designated 16th century. Records would indicate that at least a similar establishment stood on this site in 1358.

Mr. & Mrs. Stevens with two of their daughters outside their shop at No. 133 High Street, Henley. The shop sold, stationery, small gift items and tobacco. Some old favourite cigarettes can be seen in the window such as Three Castles, Gold Flake, Star.

Mr. Stevens was by profession a printer, his works being over the shop. His last surviving daughter, Katie lived in the later years of her life at No. 155 High Street, where she died in 1987.

The George & Dragon Inn.
121 High Street.

Records say that this building could be 16th century but the ornate woodwork on the front was an addition in this century. This Inn is mentioned in connection with the St. Johns Lodge of Freemasons who had their meetings here in 1797. The new De Montfort Lodge was constituted in 1929 and today hold their meetings at the Guildhall. Today the property is used for office accommodation. In the 60's it was the private residence of Mr. & Mrs. C. Slingsby, High Bailiff 1964/1965.

Stone House.

Was built towards the end of the 18th century, is now occupied by an old established firm of solicitors, G. F. Lodder & Sons. It has served as the telephone exchange, post office as well as an asylum.

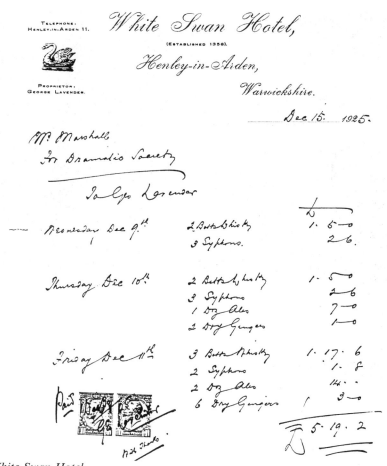

White Swan Hotel
*In addition to the interesting prices of liquid refreshments it would appear that an
Inn was established in 1358.*

The Chemist Shop.
135 High Street.
Records show that a Pharmacy establishment has existed on this site
from the year 1830. It is estimated that the building was constructed
towards the end of the 17th century. A Mr. W. F. Hopkins opened it in
1830 and remained for 40 years. His successor was a Mr. Frederick
Johnson who served his apprenticeship with Mr. Hopkins. Mr. Johnson
retired in 1890 but continued to live in the area until his death in 1903.
His attachment to Henley is reflected by his very generous gift of money

Hopkins, outside of which stands a pony and trap is the chemist. Mr. Hopkins retired in 1870. The shop on the right belonged to Mr. Herring.

for the erection of a block of almshouses, which bear his name and show the date 1904. These houses are situated at the north end of the town. From 1890 until 1896 the business went through a period of indifferent management and was finally purchased from the official receiver by a Mr. F. B. Wooddisse of Kenilworth. This gentleman obtained the services of a Mr. T. R. Perkins who managed the business on his behalf, before purchasing the business himself. Mr. Perkins retired on health grounds in 1945. One of his hobbies was a keen interest in railways, he frequently contributed articles to the Railway Magazine. He claimed to be the only person to have travelled over every inch of railway line that was used for passenger traffic throughout the British Isles. Mr. Perkins' assistant was Jack Willoughby, a quiet man but most consciencious, he came from Norfolk. He first came to Henley following his discharge from the Army in 1919 in answer to an advert by Mr. Perkins for an assistant. Jack Willoughby continued to live in Henley after his retirement until his death in 1988.

Ye olde Bank House.
137 High Street.
Now a restaurant for Indian cuisine. In the early part of the 19th century Richard Burman bought this property for his drapery business. At about the same time he became the Henley agent for a Stratford banking house. The two businesses appear to have prospered until Richard Burmans death in 1850 when his son took over. We next learn that about 1870 the

Stourbridge & Kidderminster bank purchased the property and carried on their business for the next twenty years, when they moved to No. 66 High Street where they remained until the Midland Bank took them over in 1914.

Barclays Bank.
143 High Street.
This building is said to be very nearly three hundred years old. Towards the end of the last century it was given to the diocese by a Miss Lea who lived at Tanworth-in-Arden. The Rev. G. Bell who had been living at the vicarage moved in with his family which consisted of ten children and stayed until his retirement in 1914.

The Guildhall.
See Court Leet.

Cross Keys Inn.
There is very little information about this establishment which was situated in Beaudesert Lane on the right hand side almost opposite the Parish Room.

The White Horse Inn.
130 High street.
Although now a private dwelling it still bears the old title over the front door. A little surprising to know that in coaching days this Inn was able to offer stabling at the rear.

The Coach & Horses Inn.
157 High Street.
Not much sign now that a drinking house once stood on this site.

The Nags Head Inn.
161 High Street.
Still very much in business after a considerable modernisation programme carried out in 1990.

The Liquor Vine Vaults.
171 High Street.
Now the site of a gentlemens' outfitters.

The Red Lion Hotel.
Still open for business in one of the narrowest parts of the High Street. Now declared redundant (1991) 1992 work has commenced to convert site for private accommodation.

The flower baskets outside 'The White Horse' (130 High Street) which Marjorie Hawkes remembers. Mr. Goddard watering each morning during the summer (Baptist Church in the background).

The Red Lion Inn with Mr. Hodges bakers shop next door, with blind drawn.

St. Johns Church (sometime before 1912). The Vicarage on right (now Barclays Bank plc). Guildhall to the left of St. Johns. Ground floor divided into two shops. (Findon Butcher, State Crockery).

147 High Street, Henley-in-Arden.

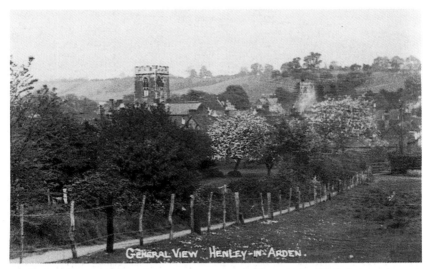

Becks Croft footpath leading from Brook End Close to the High Street.

Now the premises of hair-dresser Bernard Rogers who is one of Henley's longest serving establishments. Mr. Arnold originally conducted his boot and shoe business from the shop which became Beck Harris' butchers shop in 1930.

Mr. Stinson's business premises to the left of milestone cottage (183 High Street).

The first opening on the right is the entrance to the rear of the Blue Bell Inn. The second opening is the entrance to what was the Tan Yard.
  To support Mr. Trinders account of Tan Yard.

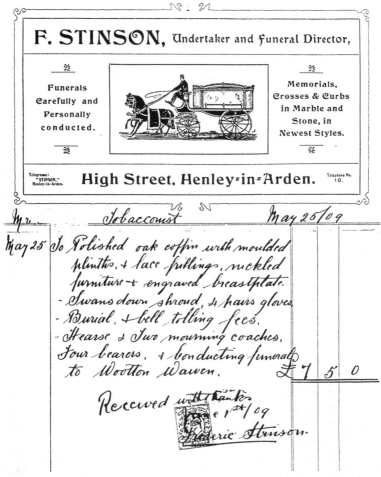

One of his accounts for the year 1909 makes interesting reading in what was available from the undertaker.

The Golden Cross Hotel.
Stands at the junction of the busy Warwick-Redditch and Stratford-Birmingham roads. Re-built at the beginning of this century.

Ice-Cream Parlour.
150 High Street.
See my conversations with Mrs. O Fathers and Beatrice Parkes.

The Golden Cross Inn, 1906.

227 High Street in use as a committee room during an election campaign.

The Coach and Pair belonged to Mr. & Mrs. Strangs who lived at the Yew Trees. They made their coach available to the hospital, which had been set up within the Public Hall, to assist in the convalescence of soldiers recovering from wounds sustained during the first World War. (outside the Golden Cross).

The Yew Trees.

A very fine 16th century property which has been altered somewhat from its original beginnings. In the late 18th century it was referred to as Yew Trees Hall. The Yew Trees from which the house takes its name are stated to have been planted in 1730.

The Central School.

Once sandwiched between the Yew Trees and the Ice Cream Parlour, it was opened in 1884, at a cost of £2834. Most of the people I have spoken to in this book started their schooling there. A number of cottages and a malthouse were demolished to make way for the new school. Whilst the interior of this building has been converted to private residences the exterior is, as far as one can tell, the same as it was in 1884.

Mrs. Hewins from the dairy with one of her customers, in New Road, Henley sometime before 1932. The Dairy was situated on the corner of High Street & School Road (now the ice cream parlour).

Corner of Ardenhouse Lane and Stratford Road. On the back of this photograph is the name, Annie Blackwell.

The Henley-in-Arden Public Hall & Institute Ltd.
(Now the Memorial Hall)

In April 1908 the above Company was formed for the purpose of building a Working Man's Club to be used for concerts, theatricals, dances, meetings and social gatherings. A suitable site off the new Station Road owned by the "Loyal Arden" Lodge of Oddfellows had been offered to the Company for the sum of £50. The Great Western Railway Company who owned the new Station Road were prepared to grant a right of access to the site in consideration of the payment of the sum of £1. per annum with a small additional sum for damage to the road. The cost of the building including the furnishing and architects fees was estimated to be £1225. The minimum subscription on which the directors were prepared to proceed was the issue of 1100 shares of £1 each. Owing to difficulties with the foundations and special expenses connected with furnishing, the total cost amounted to £1600. The extra costs were met from the issue of additional shares. The Hall was opened at the beginning of 1909.

During the first World War, 1914-1918, the Hall was used as a reception centre for wounded soldiers.

After the war the Hall reverted to its former use.

The following extracts are taken from copies of original poster advertising shows given in the Public Hall. It would appear that to coincide with the opening evening performance The Great Western Railway were prepared to run special services.

Opening performance

January 4th 1909. at 2.30 p.m.
Oscar Asche and Lily Brayton
in one or more scenes from
"The Taming of the Shrew"
as played by them over 600 times in
London and the provinces.
Reserved seats 3/- and 2/-, unreserved seats 1/-.
Gallery 6d.

January 5th at 7.30 p.m.
"Compromising Martha."
A comedy in one act by
Keble Howard (J. Keble Bell)

THE NEW

Public Hall and Institute,

HENLEY-IN-ARDEN.

——••••——

OPENING PERFORMANCES

Monday Afternoon, January 4th, at 2-30.

Tuesday Evening, January 5th, at 7-30.

Wednesday Evening, January 6th, at 7-30.

———

PRICES OF ADMISSION—

At Opening Performance on Monday Afternoon, January 4th.

RESERVED SEATS **3/-** AND **2/-.**

UNRESERVED SEATS **1/-.**   GALLERY **6d.**

(Doors open at 2 o'clock.)

At Evening Performances on January 5th and 6th.

RESERVED SEATS **2/6.**

UNRESERVED SEATS **1/-.**   GALLERY **6d.**

(Doors open at 7 o'clock).

———

Seats may be booked on and after Tuesday, December 1st, at MR. ROBERT HERRING'S, 98, High Street, Henley-in-Arden, where plans of the Hall may be seen.

Applications by post may also be addressed to MR. ROBERT HERRING and will be promptly attended to, but must in all cases be accompanied by a remittance.

Intending visitors are requested to apply for seats early, as the accommodation is limited.

Oscar Asche and Lily Brayton

In one or more Scenes from

The Taming of the Shrew

As played by them over 600 times in London and the Provinces.

—— ——

At Opening Performance on Monday Afternoon, Jan. 4th only.

Compromising Martha.

A COMEDY IN ONE ACT

by

KEBLE HOWARD

(J. KEBLE BELL).

As played at the Haymarket Theatre for 245 performances.

as played at the Haymarket Theatre for 245 performances
The part of the Curate will be played by
Keble Howard (The author)
Supported by a specially selected
professional London Company

January 6th at 7.30 p.m.
"Trial by Jury"
A dramatic Cantata.
Written by W. S. Gilbert
Composed by Arthur Sullivan.
(by permission of Mrs. D'Oyly Carte)
Will be produced by a Company of well known local amateurs.

Seats for the two evening performances Reserved 2/6d. Unreserved 1/-.
Gallery 6d.

Great Western Railway
Special Train Service.

for evening performances on January 5th & 6th.
Depart. Stratford-on-Avon. 6.45 p.m.
(stopping Wilmcote & Wootton Wawen)
Arrive Henley-in-Arden 7.7 p.m.
Depart Henley-in-Arden 11 p.m.
(stopping Wootton Wawen and Wilmcote)
Arrive Stratford-on-Avon. 11.22 p.m.
January 5th only train will leave Henley-in-Arden 10.35 p.m.
for Lapworth and Knowle (the original railway line)
A train leaves Henley-in-Arden each evening at 10.41 p.m.
for Birmingham via Tyseley stopping at all stations
on the way arriving Birmingham 11.40 p.m.

Thursday March 25th 1909 at 8 o'clock
Concert of Sacred Song.
Artists.

Soprano	*Contralto*
Miss Nellie Finch	Miss Ida M Ryley.
(Birmingham Town Hall Concerts)	(Birmingham Select Choir)

Tenor
Mr. Leonard Brown.
(Birmingham and Lancashire Choral Societies Concerts)

The Filbert Cafe with the recently completed Public Hall in the back ground (1910).

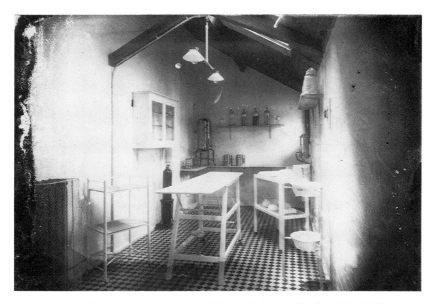

The operating Theatre in use at the Public Hall during the first World War.

Milly Chalmers Mother helping in the kitchen at the Public Hall sometime during the first World War.

Outside the Public Hall, Henley-in-Arden sometime during the first World War.

PROGRAMME

OF

ENTERTAINMENT

ARRANGED BY

The Arden Habitation of the
Primrose League.

THE PUBLIC HALL, HENLEY-IN-ARDEN,

On Tuesday, May 25th, 1909,

AT 8 O'CLOCK.

PROPRIETORS:
The Henley-in-Arden Public Hall and Institute Ltd.
MANAGING DIRECTOR: MR. W. ERNEST NELSON.

PUBLIC HALL, HENLEY-IN-ARDEN.

Proprietors:
THE HENLEY-IN-ARDEN PUBLIC HALL & INSTITUTE LTD.
Managing Director: MR. W. ERNEST NELSON.

Concert of Sacred Song

THURSDAY, MARCH 25, 1909, AT 8 O'CLOCK.

Artistes:
SOPRANO: CONTRALTO:
MISS NELLIE FINCH   MISS IDA M. RYLEY
(Birmingham Town Hall Concerts)   (Birmingham Select Choirs)

TENOR:
MR. LEONARD BROWN
(Birmingham and Lancashire Choral Societies Concerts)

BARITONE:
MR. DOUGLAS WAKEFIELD.
(Late Theatre Royal Drury Lane, and George Edwardes's Companies)

Solo Violin   ...   ...   MR. W. VICKERSTAFF.
Accompanists   MR. FRANK MORTON & MR. WALTER STAIT.

PART 1.

1. VOCAL DUET   "Tenor and Baritone"   ... Lane Wilson.
    MESSRS COX AND INGRAM.
2. SONG   ...   " Awake"   ...   Pelissier
    MISS RUTH BELL.
3. MONOLOGUE ...   "A Fallen Star"   ...   Chevalier.
    MR. CLEMENT BAKER.
4. VIOLIN SOLO ...   "Serenade" Angelique"   ... Lewis Hann
    MISS GRACE WHITWORTH.
5. SONG   ...   "The Drum Major"   ... Ernest Newton
    MR. LEONARD COX.
6. SONG   ...   "Chorus Gentlemen"   ...   Lohr
    MR. RALPH INGRAM.
7. SONG   ...   "La Serenata"   ...   Braga
    MISS R. BELL: Violin Obligato MISS G. WHITWORTH.
8. SONG   ...   "Three for Jack"   ... W. H. Squire
    MR. LEONARD COX.
9. SONG   ...   "The Jolly Sailor"   ...   Airlie Dix
    MR. RALPH INGRAM.
10. HUMOROUS SONG "Wot vov do 'ee luv 'oi'   Chevalier
    MR. CLEMENT BAKER.

ACCOMPANIST   ...   MR. FRANCIS MORTON.

An Address will be given by

PHILIP S. FOSTER ESQ., M.P.

PART II.

"POOR PILLICODDY"

A FARCE,

IN ONE ACT, BY J. H. MORTON.

CHARACTERS.

Mr. Pillicoddy ... (a Nurseryman) ... MR. C. H. HENNIKER.
Captain O'Scuttle   ...   .   MR. C. W. FALCON.
Mrs. Pillicoddy ...   .   MRS. J. E. MITCHELL.
Mrs. O'Scuttle ...   .   MISS RAHILLY.
Sarah Blunt...   ...   .   MISS RYLAND.

SCENE:

A Room in Pillicoddy's House adjoining the Nursery
Gardens.

God Save the King.

Baritone
Mr. Douglas Wakefield.
(late Theatre Royal, Drury Lane & George Edwardes's Companies)

Tuesday May 15th 1909 at 8 o'clock
Poor Pillicoddy.
a farce
In one act by J. H. Morton.

Monday & Tuesday 7/8th February, 1910
Pirates of Penzance.
'or the slave of duty'
The well known comic opera in two acts.
Doors open at 7.30 p.m. Commence at 8 o'clock
(carriages at 10)

Monday Evening March 27th 1911
Mr William A. Clark.
will give a lecture illustrated with
Lime light Views entitled
"Some thoughts on our English Cathedrals"
This lecture has proved very popular and the
Lantern Slides used are the entire work of the Lecturer.
Admission 2d.
Members of the Institute free.

Monday November 6th 1911 at 7.45 p.m.
Dramatic Performance
Mr. H. R. Allinson's Company in:-
"A Tight Corner"
A farcial Comedy in 3 acts by Herbert Swears.

Dramatis Personae.

Jack Hyacinth a young Stock-broker	Mr. Harry Allinson
Sampson Quayle his friend	Mr. Harold Howell
Barrington Skews	Mr. Horace A. Evans
Hall ⎫ (The men from Dentons)	Mr. Leonard Gough
Green ⎭	Mr. Holbrook
Mrs. Pertwee	Miss Wilhelmine Bocker
Clara, Maid to Mrs. Hyacinth	Miss Maria Rice
Mrs. Jack Hyacinth	Miss Adelina Mabbett

at the Piano Mrs. Fred Harris

Presented by
Royal Society for the Prevention of Cruelty to Animals.
A popular Lantern Lecture
(Illustrated with Lime Light Views)
by Miss Constance Warner.

Monday March 11th 1912 at 8 p.m.
Admission Free.
Children not admitted under 14.

Thursday January 30th 1913
Mrs. Dot.
A comedy in 3 Acts.
by W. Somerset Maughan.

Tuesday Evening April 15th 1913
Grand Entertainment
In aid of the Claverdon Boy's Scouts.
Reserved seats 2/-. Unreserved 1/-. and 6d. Gallery 6d.
Doors open at 7.30 p.m. to commence at 8 o'clock.

Part 1

1. Pianoforte Solo   Mrs Fred Harris
2. Song   'Be Prepared'   The Scouts
3. Rag-time duet   'Pucker up your lips Miss Lindy'   Messrs. Taylor & Banks
4. Song   'A Surmise'   Mr. Frank Lester
5. Song   'Stop your Tickling Jock'   Mr. Ben Wakefield
6. Recitation   'One legged Goose'   Miss Effie Wakefield
7. Comic Song   'The Shoe Black'   Mr. Oliver James
8. Rag Time Duet   'All aboard for Alabama'   Messrs Taylor & Banks.

Part 2

1. Pianoforte Solo   Mrs Fred Harris
2. Song   The Chief   The Scouts
3. Song   'We parted on the shore'   Mr Ben Wakefield
4. Rag-time duet   'Dixie'   Messrs. Taylor & Banks
5. Song   'The Young Loyalist'   Mr. Frank Lester
6. Comic Song   (The Light House Keeper)   Mr. Oliver James
7. Whistling Song   Messrs. Taylor & Banks

The entertainment will conclude with a special sketch, entitled
'On the track of the Spies'
(by kind permission of the Editor of the Scout)
Performed entirely by the Boy Scouts.

Wednesday February 11th 1914
Programme of Dramatic Performance
by the members of the Shirley Institute Dramatic Society
'Are you a Mason'
A farcical Comedy.

Saturday 11th October 1919
The National Federation of Discharged
and Demobilised Sailors & Soldiers.
Henley-in-Arden Branch.
A Concert.
The Birmingham Soldiers Concert Party
have kindly consented to attend
and will render a varied programme

Price of admission will be
Front seats 2/-. Second seats 1/-. Gallery 6d.

The above charges do not include the Amusement Tax which will be
charged at the door and added to the previously purchased tickets.

Thursday March 31st 1921

Warriors Day.
Entertainment
at the
PUBLIC HALL
HENLEY-IN-ARDEN
All seats on floor of hall may be booked in advance at
2/6d. 2/-. & 1/-.
at the Henley-in-Arden Post Office.
Gallery 1/-. unreserved.
for further particulars see large bills.
THIS IS NOT A CHARITY — IT IS A DUTY
I hope to see every seat in the Hall occupied.

Signed. W. Ernest Nelson.
High Bailiff.

In 1946 following a number of public meetings the Public Hall & Institute
Ltd. was taken over by 'The Henley-in-Arden War Memorial Trust' to the
memory of those Towns-people who laid down their lives and to those who
rendered service to their Country during the World War 1939 – 1945. The
Hall still exists for the same objectives which inspired its erection back in
1908.

In 1947 the property and funds known and belonging to the Henley-in-Arden Public Hall & Institute Ltd were legally transferred and would in future be known as The Henley-in-Arden War Memorial Trust which is dedicated to the memory of those Townspeople who laid down their lives and those who rendered service to their Country during the World War 1939/1945. The original trustees proposed to facilitate the transfer and registration under the official Trustee of Charity Lands were:-

Harry Norman Welch. Patrick John Garland.
James Leek. The Rev. Albert Henry Webb.

After the completion of this procedure the Henley-in-Arden War Memorial Trust was and is administered by committees of townspeople and representatives from organisations within the town.

HENLEY-IN-ARDEN V.A. AUXILIARY HOSPITAL
OPENED NOVEMBER 28th 1914
CLOSED APRIL 5th 1919

The Hospital started in 1914 with 22 beds, and ended in 1919 with 82 beds, 52 being at Henley-in-Arden and 30 at Wootton Hall. During this long period, the hospital was not closed for a single day, and also holds the record of having been open for a longer period than any other Auxiliary Hospital attached to the First Southern General Hospital.

The number of patients treated was 1576, with only 2 deaths; and 50 or 60 per cent of the cases taken were "cot" cases.

The Wootton Hall Extension was opened in June 1917 through the kindness of Mr & Mrs Guinness, who fitted up part of their beautiful home as a hospital for the wounded. This extention proved of the greatest benefit to the Henley-in-Arden Hospital, as it enabled cases to be transferred direct to that building.

The Henley-in-Arden Open Air Ward was the first of the kind to be introduced. The larger Open Air Ward, known as Muntz Ward, with the Administrative Block, was the generous gift of Mr. F. E. Muntz, of Umberslade, in the early days of 1917.

These buildings were given and removed to The County Tuberculosis Hospital Bramcote, near Nuneaton, where they formed an annexe. The wards retained their old names of the Henley-in-Arden Open Air Ward, and the Henley-in-Arden Muntz Ward, and was of benefit to many poor soldiers and civilians who were unfortunate enough to contract this terrible disease.

The following is a list of those who served with the V.A.Ds Warwick Nos. 11 and 32 during the first World War. (18 members served during the whole period, viz from Nov. 1914 to April 5th, 1919).

W. Ernest Nelson. O.B.E.	Commandant and Medical Officer.
Rose G. Nelson	Assistant Commandant.
Lydia Guinness	Hon. Ass. Commandant (Wootton Hall Extension).
N. Stevenson A.R.R.C.	Matron.
P. F. Lodder	Lady Superintendent.
Amy F. Cox	Quartermaster.
Joyce Agar	Quartermaster.

W. Dawes	Quartermaster and Pack Store Master.
H. H. Munro	Quartermaster and Pack Store Master.
T. R. Perkins	Pharmacist.
K. Wilcox	Night Sister.
E. L. Hawkes	Relief Sister.
Lillian Heynes	Masseuse.
G. F. Lodder	Auditor.
A. L. Robbins	Secretary.
Rev. F. D. Lane M.A.	Chaplain.

V.A. NURSES

A. Albrighton	M. Avery	E. K. Bagshaw	N. Belcher	A. Blackwell
L. Brettell	R. Dodd	V. Daly	V. Grazebrook	M. Guinness
L. Hands	M. Hemming	M. Jamieson	F. Kirby	M.Lively
G. Moncrieff	D. Moore	M. Moore	G. Richards	C. M. Ryland
M. Sladen	B. Steele	E. Strang	L. Teece	R. Wakefield
L. Whitehead	W. Wright			

V.A. COOKS

A. Atkins	A. Coldicott	H. Crookes	Q. Davis	M. Dixon
Mabel Dixon	E. Hackwood	C. Hartley	M. J. Hawkes	I. Herring
T. Heynes	M. Stephens	E. C. Stephens		

V.A. ORDERLIES (Women)

R. K. Baker	A. Bonberry	D. Crisp	R. Stracey Clitherow,
G. Collins	G. E. Cooper	H. Edkins	E. Hawkes
F. A. Hazlewood	L. Hirons	A. Hodgkins	P. K. Kitching
D. des Longrais	H. P. Newcombe	S. Owens	D. Robertson
D. Saunders	G. Taylor		

Men's DETACHMENT

O. James	F. Stinson	(Section	A. R. Jenner
F. Bioletti	G. A. Dalby	Leaders)	(Sergt.)
B. Sly	L. Stanton	W. Hadley	H. Hodges
W. Eccles	F. W. Hemming	J. V. Watkins	G. Coppage
L. Watkins		W. Sly	R. Turner

Henley-in-Arden Residents

Charles Hubert Beech
Una May Beech

Mrs. Beech.

I was born on the 7th March, 1905 at Alne Hills, some three miles from Great Alne. I weighed 1½ lbs. at birth. My mother kept me in a cot in front of the fire, this was in the days before there was such things as incubators. I did not go to school until I was 7 and left at 14. To get to school I had to walk nearly three miles to Great Alne. If the weather was too bad we stayed away. We took sandwiches to school for lunch and during the winter we took dried Cocoa and the teachers would make us a hot drink. Lighting in our cottage was by oil which was delivered by a man who called without fail once a week.

He would carry on his cart all sorts of things that you might want for washing and cleaning. Another person who called came from Studley, selling clothes. My grandfather always kept two pigs and my father grew almost all our vegetables so we never really went short of food. There was never a lot at Christmas, perhaps a rag doll, a sugar pig, and a sugar clock. When I left school I went into service at Alcester. Round about 1921 my parents moved to Bishopton.

Mr. Beech.

I was born on the 1st January 1905 at Bearley. Went to the local school, happy days. I was known as Buck, still am, but I never knew where the name came from. We were never really hungry because we had plenty of solid food, suet puddings and the like. As lads we would often dig a carrot or a swede out of a field and cut them up and eat them.

Christmas time you perhaps would make do with a piece of wood shaped like a horse with four cotton reels on the legs which meant you could push or pull it. I would be about 11/12 years when there was a terrific thunderstorm and I can remember a flash of lightning striking our grandfather clock and making a shower of sparks. When I left school at 14 I worked on a number of local farms until in 1925 when I was 20 years I joined Warwickshire County Council. Round about this time I met my wife. She was cycling on the main road from Stratford, I was with a number of other lads by the Golden Cross at Bearley. As she came by I called out "where you be going," she said 'to see my Granny', I said "I'll come with you." I rode part of the way with her and arranged to meet her the following Sunday, but I forgot.

The following Sunday she came along and we began courting until we were married on the 25th June, 1927 at Bishopton Church, since demolished. On the day of the wedding my best man and I cycled over from Bearley to the Church. We left our cycles in the hedge. My wife only lived a few hundred yards from the Church so she and her family walked. We went back to her place for a meal. Afterwards we got our bikes and cycled to Henley, where I had rented a cottage. It rained all the way but we were as happy as a pair of crickets, no honeymoon for us.

We only stayed in this cottage for a few weeks before we moved into a cottage in the Tan Yard, in Henley. We were there for thirty years. We had a living room and two bedrooms. The toilet and wash house was at the bottom of the yard. The property was owned by a Mrs. Slater. Later we moved into a bungalow, still in the Tan Yard which had a kitchen, pantry and three bedrooms. Before people lived in the Tan Yard it had been used for tanning leather.

Mrs. Beech.
The beams were still exposed where the leather was hung. Something I shall always remember whilst at the Tan Yard was seeing a man whose hair was standing up on end — he lived next door and had gone mad. He was taken to Hatton Asylum. I worked for a Mrs. Hartley for 42 years, she lived on the High Street, just round from the Tan Yard, next to the Blue Bell Inn. I worked at this Inn at weekends. Mrs. Hartley before she was married was a Miss Balken. Her father was connected with the London stage.

We have never been away on holiday, we never saw the fun in paying others to look after us, when you needed the money yourself.

Mr. Beech.
It would not suit me to have my legs under somebody else's table.

On the council we started at 6.30 a.m. and worked until 5.30 p.m. for 6/-. a day. You could be working at places like Binton, Hampton-in-Arden, Catherine-De-Barnes but you still had to be there by 6.30 a.m. and you only had the old bike to get you there. If you were late the foreman would stand you off until 9 a.m. which would cost you a shilling or two from your wages. In the summer of 1925 it was particularly hot and dry for a long period. The lakes at Earlswood had dried up and we had to go to the canal at Wilmcote to pump water by hand into four wheel carts for the use of the Steam Rollers. In those days I remember that cutting the grass verges was done by a man pulling the mower and another man to guide it.

I took my test to drive a steam roller at Wroxhall, I have the certificate dated 6th September, 1938. I enjoyed my work on those old steam rollers, it was dirty work mind you. In the winter months you kept warm but in the summer months the old feet got warm. The Council changed to diesel rollers in about 1948 and they were cold things in the winter. For about thirty years I would take for my dinner two thick slices of bread and some fat bacon in between. Not only did I eat this at work but I would eat fat bacon between bread for my tea on Saturdays and Sundays and loved it.

Mrs. Beech.
We moved to this house in Cherry Orchard in November 1957. We spent 30 years at the Tan Yard and we have been here now over 30 years. We celebrated our Diamond Wedding on the 25th June, 1987.

Mr Beech died on the 27th February 1991.

Ada Mildred Chalmers (nee Hodges)

I was born on the 17th May, 1898 in the cottage to the left of the Blue Bell Inn, Henley. My grandfather Hodges worked as a gardener for the Nelson family who lived at Feckenham, Worcestershire and had decided to move to Henley-in-Arden. They asked him to come with them, which he did. I would think this was about 1870 because my father was apparently a baby in arms when the family moved to Henley and he was 91 when he died in 1959.

My mother came from Lapworth and died in 1948.

I was nearly one year old when my parents moved to No. 110 High Street. The property had been an old farmhouse; it had four bedrooms and two attics. My parents lived there for 47 years before moving across the road to the Guildhall cottage. My father was a member of the Court Leet and he had just retired when the Steward of the Court offered him the position of caretaker and gardener. My father was very keen to accept but my mother did not really want to leave her old home where she had lived for so long, however they went. This would be sometime in the early forties.

One of my earliest memories is of being ill just before Christmas, I would be about four at the time. I learned later that I had had Pneumonia. Granny Sly as we called her was both nurse and midwife. She came in to see me and told my mother to call the doctor immediately. I remember her for the print dresses she wore together with her spotless white apron. In addition to the medicine Doctor Nelson prescribed he suggested to my mother than I should have green welsh flannel next to my chest under what we called a chemise. I wore this each winter for a number of years. Another nurse was Granny Horsley.

One of the things my mother promised me if I would take my medicine was a doll's pram. After I was better I would look out each day for my pram. One day I was out with my elder brother Edgar when I saw the railway horse drawn covered cart draw up by our house. I was very excited and said to my brother I am sure that will be my pram. It turned out that it was. I remember it was painted green. I was so proud of it. I can see my brother carrying my pram across the road to ensure that the wheels did not get dirty. About this time I printed a letter of thanks to Dr. Nelson which my mother pinned over my bed. When the doctor read the letter he thanked me and gave me a sixpenny piece.

I went to school on the High Street, between Milking Lane and School Road, there was no school road in those days. Mrs. Argyle was head teacher of the Infants section which had two classes. One day a Mr. Bromborough came to our school, who I now know was a retired head teacher. He came into our classroom and I can remember Mrs Argyle saying 'stand up Daddy Long Legs' — that was because I was very tall. My father went to what they called the British School which stood where Charles Phillips the estate agents have their offices (44 High Street). He would take 2d. a week with him to pay for his schooling. We always wore a pinafore to go to school in. Our day always commenced with Hymns and Prayers followed by a scripture lesson. Next was Arithmetic then English, Geography and History. We also had a Violin class, you paid a 1/-. a week towards the cost of the Violin: My brother Edgar joined this class but not me. We did not have school reports but we did receive prizes for coming top of the class and for good attendance. Our prizes would be books.

My father always seemed to have one pig which he kept at the top of the garden. We had a metal bowl which we used for washing up, this water was always kept for the pig because of the amount of grease it would contain. My mother would insist that after the bowl had been used it had to be cleaned both inside and outside. We always kept the small potatoes for the pig, they were boiled in the copper. As children we loved to get hold of one of these small potatoes after they had been boiled, they always seemed to taste so much better than oridinary boiled potatoes. After the pig had been killed the various joints would hang up round the kitchen, this was after salt had been well rubbed in.

As I have already mentioned my mother's family lived in Lapworth. To visit our grandmother we would go by train from Henley Old Station, this was before the North Warwickshire line was built and go to Kingswood as I believe Lapworth station was called in those days. For some reason I never discovered we were never allowed to go into my grandmothers front room or her pantry. The grocer, I remember, only called once a fortnight and sometimes the cake we were given was very stale. In the garden stood a water pump which we loved pumping. In bluebell time the garden was a picture.

When the railway line from Henley to Birmingham and Stratford was completed my mother perhaps once a year would take us to one of the exhibitions at Bingley Hall. This was a great treat because we would come home laden with leaflets, booklets and small samples.

I believe I am right in saying that I was one of those who travelled on the first train to Stratford-on-Avon, it was a Sunday school outing, only half a day. At this time we had a man lodging with us who was a foreman bricklayer, he worked on the railway and had worked on the railway bridge which took the line over New Road. When he heard about our trip to Stratford he said that he was not sure whether this bridge was safe. Of course he was only joking but my mother got terribly worried.

Another Sunday school outing was to Yarningale Common. We were taken there on Mr. Harris's coal cart, of course it had been washed down and we all sat on the floor. On the trip we went through a ford we all thought this was marvellous. Mr. Harris had his depot at the old railway station.

I cannot be sure what year it would be when the railway ran one of their first excursions from Henley. I would be about eleven so that would be 1909, it was to Weymouth. We were all so excited to be going to the sea-side because none of us had ever seen the sea. The train left Henley at 4 o'clock in the morning. There were plenty of people on the train which had come from Birmingham. My father did not come with us, it was years after before he could be persuaded to go on holiday. My mother used to say that he was afraid that Henley would run away if he left it. When we arrived in Weymouth, mother took us down to the beach where she placed my eldest brother in charge of the two youngest whilst she and I went off to get some apartments, as they were called in those days. We finally got fixed up and we used to take our own food in which the land-lady would cook, for us. We were away for four days. It was before the first World War that on Bank Holidays my mother would offer teas, bread and butter to visitors for 9d. The visitors came mainly from Birmingham. In addition she would offer bunches of flowers from our garden for 6d. I loved to count the money at the end of the day.

Years ago we seemed to have quite a lot of bakers. There was Mr. Badger who had his shop where Beechcroft is today. Whenever you asked him how he was he would always reply 'pretty middling'. There was another baker at no. 74 High Street. There was one at the Bank House 'Eccles' in addition to baking they would cater for parties, some of these would even come from Birmingham. The parties were held in a shed down Beaudesert Lane on the right hand side just beyond the river.

On some adjoining ground they had a little fair ground with swings and roundabouts. Then there was Welch's right in the middle of the High Street. At the bottom of the High Street, next to the Red Lion, my Uncle Jim and Auntie Kit kept a bakers' shop. My Uncle had a very good name for his Cottage Loaves. My Auntie would tell us a story told to her by Granny Edkins who said she often woke up during the night to hear carts passing through from the direction of Wootton carrying bodies which had been dug up from the churchyard there. She went on to say that these men were called 'body snatchers' and sold the bodies for medical research.

Mr. Lot Robinson was our head teacher. Games we played were skipping, farmer in his den, not certain how that went. Another game was that we form a circle then one girl would walk round the outside of the circle and then drop a handkerchief behind someone who would have to pick it up and try and catch the girl before she returned to her place, if she didn't then she would repeat what the previous girl had done. We had spinning tops which we would press into the soil between the cobbles which were set between the curb and paving sets. You would get yourself a stick and tie a piece of string on to make yourself a whip to get your top spinning but you did have to be careful not to send your top through someone's window.

Our schooling was mainly concerned with learning the three 'R's. May 24th was Empire Day. We would celebrate by saluting the Union Jack which was flying from a flag pole which stood in a small fenced off area in front of the school. We would sing 'what is the meaning of Empire Day' then 'God Save the King' and then end up with a half days holiday. Occasionally my brother and I would save up 6d. between us and then go to Mr. Newcombe and hire one of his bikes for an hour. We used to take it in turns to ride up and down Beaudesert Lane, my mother insisted that we had to be where she could keep an eye on us.

In one of the cottages close to the Golden Cross lived a Katie Wren who was quite a character. She had a Jackdaw who would sit at her table. She never went anywhere without her two crutches, although she hardly never made use of them to support herself. One day Mr. Wilkes the carrier who lived at 261 High Street, was passing on his way to Stratford when Katie came running out calling for Mr. Wilkes to stop whilst she went back for her crutches.

On the other side of the road almost opposite where Katie lived was a row of cottages which were called Chingley Bank, where De-Montford Court now stands. In one of these lived a Mrs Coates with her son Harry. They carried out a variety of jobs, plucking fowl, shoe repairs even chiropody. If I ever took any shoes for repair I was always hopeing that Mrs Coates would ask me to take them through to the shed at the back which served as her son's workshop. By going through the house I had the chance of seeing a glass case under which there was a stuffed cat and three kittens. I always wanted to stay and gaze at this case with its strange contents.

I left school when I was fourteen to take a job with Dr. Brown who lived at Minchinhampton, near Stroud, Glos. He had married one of the Rev. G. Bells, (one time Rector of Henley) daughters. I went to train as a child's nurse. I was not there long because I was not happy at living away from home. After a few months a school friend of mine suggested we sit for an examination at the Shire Hall, Warwick, for the position of pupil teachers. We took the exam. and both of us passed. We were required to report to the school in Henley where we had both been pupils. Mr. Robinson the head teacher had us report at 8 o'clock in the morning, although school did not start until 9 o'clock. The extra hour was to prepare for opening lessons. A

Mrs. Wood came once a week to instruct my friend and I in the art of teaching. She was a very nice person. For the rest of the week we reported to Mr. Robinson and he instructed us and gave us the opportunity of quietening the children down when they came into the classroom. This instruction went on for four years. At the end of this period my friend and I took a further exam. which we both passed. My friend was sent to Salter Street School (Earlswood) and I to the Church School for girls at Solihull, next to the Parish Church. The Great War was in progress at this time.

One of my memories was sitting with my mother looking out of our front window for what she called 'the grease van'. This was a van drawn by four horses which belonged to Warriner & Mason the grocery wholesalers of Birmingham. This van brought butter, margarine and lard amongst other grocery items to the small grocers shop which was next door (now Gateways). As soon as the van had gone my mother would run round to the shop and buy whatever the grocer would allow her to have. These fats were not rationed as they were in World War 2. For our tea my mother would only allow us to have butter on one slice of bread and jam only on the other slice. I would rub the jammed piece lightly against the buttered piece which meant that I did have a little of both butter and jam on both slices. Sometimes we had lard on toast and jam on toast. My mother made all her own jam.

I spent five very happy years at the Solihull school before I got married. To get to Solihull I went by train from Henley to Shirley then I biked to Solihull. I lodged with an Uncle in Solihull during the week, returning home on the Friday evening for the weekend. There were occasions whilst cycling when it would be raining; when I arrived at school there was a lady cleaner who wore what was called a curtain bonnet made of a cotton material and she would always enquire whether I had got wet. She would be concerned that in later life I would suffer from rheumatism. Another memory from those days was of another teacher who was so concerned that the school authorities who were C of E might find out that she was a member of the Baptist Church and dismiss her. She later married a man some years younger than herself. He was apparently very keen on walking and cycling. She again became very worried as to whether she would be able to keep up with him as they got older. Her worries were never put to the test because unfortunately she was killed riding her cycle after being in collision with a car driven by a woman from Henley.

I married in 1921. Living so close to St. Johns Church we walked across the road to Church. Our first home was at No. 13 Cherry Orchard. Although there was not a lot of money coming in we always managed to have a week's holiday at Weston.

Whilst I was a founder member of the Henley-in-Arden W.I. I had previously been attending the Wootton Wawen W.I. with an aunt of mine. Some of our earliest meeting at Wootton were at the Mill and I think some were held at Wootton Hall. Mrs. Guinness who lived there was a member of

Wootton W.I. As soon as I heard that a W.I. was to be formed in Henley I put my name down and so became a founder member. Our first meeting was in the Guildhall in October 1927 under the chairmanship of Mrs. Haddlesey who lived at Tanworth-in-Arden. She later came to live at the Poplars' in Henley. People I can remember being present at our first meeting was the representative from W.I. headquarters in Leamington, Mrs. Rotherham, then Mrs. Willoughby Agar, Mrs. Lodder, Mrs. Mason (Gordon's mother) my own mother, Mrs. Cave, Mrs. Nancy Warwick, Mrs. Croft and a policeman's wife, Mrs. Robinson.

At Christmas we had a super party beautifully laid out. Everything on the menu had been prepared by the members. After the meal we had games. I was expecting my daughter Barbara at this time and I was very fond of dates. The members kept feeding me with these dates with a comment that when my baby was born she would be covered in dates. Of course she never was. Mrs. Billington was our first secretary; I later took over this office and served for 21 consecutive years, I thoroughly enjoyed this period of my life. I have also been President twice.

After our Christmas party we always had a party for the children. I used to be given £1 to buy presents with. I would go with Mrs. Woodward to Woolworths in Birmingham where we would buy 40 presents with this single £1. Mr. Clackett, a member's husband, was our Father Christmas. Even today I meet some of the people who were children in those days and remind me of those parties.

I cannot remember the year but my daughter was only a little girl, when all the institutes in Warwickshire joined together in presenting a wonderful pageant at Warwick Castle. My mother and I doubled for the part Capult, cannot remember the play. Mr H. Hawkes was Prospero from Tempest. Mrs. Mason who kept the drapers shop was Calaban. The show lasted for a week. The singing of Jerusalem at the beginning of the weeks' pageant was marvellous.

Gwen Lally was the organiser and did a wonderful job. There were crowds at every performance.

Mrs. Woodward and a Mrs. Bourne would during the second World War stand in a queue for margarine to enable us to have a few cakes for our refreshments on W.I. nights. We carried on through the war years making jam with special allocations of sugar but I cannot remember where the jam was sent.

Concerts have always been a part of W.I. The memorial hall would be filled on these occasions. We also had outings, I remember one to London, a Miss Miller organised it. When we arrived in London she did not want any of us to get out in case we got lost. We got out eventualy and I don't remember anyone getting lost. It was also a great occasion to represent your W.I. branch at the A.G.M. which used to be held at the Albert Hall. I went twice.

We have held our meetings in a variety of places, Guildhall, Parish

Room, Welch's Bakery there was a room at the rear of the shop and of course the Public Hall, now the Memorial Hall. I have known the time when we have had as many as 161 entries in our flower show. We would also organise all sorts of little competitions, for example six prettiest buttons, my most treasured ornament etc. Through our efforts we have been able to contribute quite useful sums of money to the Memorial Hall to help in its up-keep. I have a note that in 1948 we handed over £99. The committee would also organise some wonderful processions. Members would dress up and we would visit surrounding villages to collect money for the hall. I can remember buying some Little Miss Muffit Print material at 4½d. a yard to make a dress for one of these processions. Ken Terry was a great worker in fund raising. Unfortunately there is not the same interest in W.I. that there was, but I have thoroughly enjoyed my 50 years with the Henley W.I. We celebrated our 50th anniversary at the Church Hall, in October 1977. In addition to myself the only other founder member who could be present was Mrs. Willoughby Agar.

Mrs Chalmers died August 6th, 1983.

Olive Farthers (nee Ribison)

I was born on the 8th September 1900 in Newcastle-on-Tyne. My father worked for Charles Parsons as a Gas Turbine engineer. We left Newcastle in 1903 for Manchester where my father had secured a position with Westinghouse. We then moved on to Southampton for a short time before returning to Manchester where we stayed until 1910. In this year we moved to Birmingham because my father had taken a new job with Cadbury's, in charge of power. Our new home was in Beaumont Road, Bourneville. I went to Bourneville School; I hope it is as good a school today as it was when I was there, I was very happy. We never used to have written examinations at the end of term, instead we had visiting inspectors — each would be responsible for a number of subjects.

I can remember one occasion when the girl who sat in the desk in front of me was on her feet and the inspector asked her 'where was Clive born'. There was a few seconds of silence because the girl did not know the answer. Sitting behind this girl I could not be seen and I whispered sufficiently loud enough for this girl to hear 'in the dust bin'. This girl burst out laughing: she was immediately called out in front of the class to give an explanation for her laughter, but she did not tell the teacher that it was something I had said which had caused her to laugh. The teacher reprimanded her for what she had done but I did not think that she should get into trouble because of something I had said, so I went out to the teacher and confessed that it was all my fault. He sent me outside the class to stand in the corridor. I am sure there was a slight smile on his face, as I left the room. Whilst I was standing in the corridor the headteacher came along and said, 'Olive why are you standing in the corridor'. I said that I thought he should ask my teacher. Here again I feel sure that when he came out of the class room there was a slight smirk on his face. Even today I have no idea what prompted me to say what I did . . .

Each Christmas we had a splendid party, and we would take home an apple and an orange and a new sixpenny piece. I left school when I was fourteen: my parents wanted me to stay on at school and sit for the Office Examination which meant that if you were successful you stood a good chance of securing a position in one of the offices at Cadbury's. I could not wait for these examinations to come round I was keen to be earning money. Without the assistance of my Mother or Father I secured a position in Cadbury's factory. My first job was to dip the cream filling into liquid chocolate using a small fork. During each working week we were required to attend school on one day, and one morning was given over to swimming instruction. We received free dental and medical treatment. After a year in the factory I sat the 'office examination' and was successful. I was instructed to attend an interview with a Miss Clara Davies. On the day I was due to attend this interview I went ill with German Measles, I was away from work for three weeks. When I did see Miss Davies she explained that all the office vacancies had been filled. After a while she said, "I will take you to see Mr. Brown, Manager of the export department." He agreed to give me a job because at that time, 1915, he was losing young men who were being called up for military service. At the end of the war these young men began to return to their former positions.

One day Mr. Brown sent for me and said that the only job he could offer me was shorthand typing. I had never done anything like this before but Mr. Brown said if I was interested in this position he could give me a month to learn shorthand. I went to Lawrences College in New Street Birmingham twice a week and at the end of a month I was given a certificate saying that I had reached a sufficient standard of efficiency which was acceptable to Mr. Brown. As a result I stayed in the Export Department until I left to get married in 1928. When I left I was presented with a Bible and a single carnation together with a certificate saying 'I had been a good servant of the Company' by Mr. Barrow Cadbury.

Mr. George Cadbury Snr. was a very kind and considerate man. Each Wednesday morning staff were invited along to the dining room, no manager could prevent you from going, where Mr. George would read a short passage from the Bible, then we would sing one verse from a hymn. Then Mr. George would give a short talk on a variety of subjects mainly on 'how to keep well'. I can remember him saying on one occasion that we should all try to have two pairs of shoes and wear them in rotation, in this way you help preserve the leather. These little talks would only last for half an hour.

Cadbury's were suppliers of cocoa powder to Ovaltine but for some reason they began to buy their cocoa requirements from a Dutch company. This was upsetting to Cadbury's who decided to introduce a competitive drink to Ovaltine which is how BourneVita originated.

I met my husband quite by chance, this was in 1924. My sister had arranged to visit a friend who lived in Rubery, Birmingham, but on the day she was due to make this visit she was unwell and it was decided that I should keep this appointment. When I arrived I was introduced to two young men who were also visiting this family. One of the subjects we talked about was tennis. I already played on the courts at Bourneville. It was agreed that we should all meet at the Bourneville tennis courts the following Thursday. On this day it rained heavily in the evening so I felt there was no point in going to the tennis courts. During the evening the two young men turned up on a motor-bike. One of these young men was Arthur Richard Farthers to whom I became engaged during 1926, he worked at the Austin Motor Works at Longbridge. In 1928 we were married at Bourneville Church. In 1930 my daughter was born.

My husband had a brother, Harry, who had gone to America to join an uncle who was involved in the electricity business and it was thought that Harry would learn the trade but it did not work out and he returned to England. After much discussion my husband agreed with his brother that they should go into business together. They eventually saw an advert for a small dairy in Henley-in-Arden which was for sale, this was in 1932. They bought this business from a Mr. & Mrs. Hewins who retired to live in Chestnut Walk, Henley. Harry and Arthur had two milk rounds, they would go out in the morning and again in the afternoon. The milk was purchased from one of the local butchers, Mr. Hawkes. One of the first things we did was to have a cold room built, then a steam boiler installed for sterilizing the milk churns. From any milk unsold we would separate the cream which was sold for 3d., 6d., 9d. & 1/6d. The skimmed milk was given away to anyone who cared to come and collect it. Any cream unsold was made into butter using a hand turned butter churn. Many of the items we produced were sold at the market held at the back of the Nag's Head, run by Charles Pearson, a farmer, who I believe came from Great Alne or that area. In fact for all our efforts we were making very little money.

Following discussions with friends and acquaintances we decided to produce Ice-cream. We secured a hand worked freezer which processed the ingredients and made them into Ice-Cream which was then transferred to a freezer unit. We bought the cornets and wafer biscuits from Faschinno's of Stechford, Birmingham. We had the shop enlarged round about 1934 so that we could serve milk shakes in one half with two or three tables set out and in the other half we sold our Ice-Cream. There has been talk of a secret recipe for the Ice-Cream but there never was, it was simply a question of using the best ingredients possible and exercising great attention to the blending of these products. The butter came from a firm in Birmingham, the cream from St. Ivel's in Somerset, which arrived at the old Henley goods station early each morning and Charles Lamb would deliver it on behalf of the railway company each morning without fail.

We used fresh strawberries whilst in season for the strawberry ice-cream otherwise we used puree. The milk we purchased from Charles Pearson, Grade A., T.B. Tested.

We entered the International competitions held at the Crystal Palace in 1935 for which we received a diploma but the highlight was undoubtedly when we won the Faschino Cup against international competition, this was in 1937 and really made our reputation. People came from as far away as Birmingham in their cars and on cycles. Traffic became congested in the High Street because people would stop their cars and eat their ice-cream, this really became quite a problem. We received an approach from the police about the hold ups in Henley so we employed two men who we put in uniform and their job was to politely ask people not to stop and eat their ice-cream in their cars in the High Street.

When war came rationing was introduced and we did, in some cases, have to use substitution ingredients, quality did suffer. There was a period of some two or three years when we did not produce any ice-cream. After the war we received restricted permits for certain ingredients which only allowed us to produce on Sundays and Wednesdays.

It was in 1959 that we sold the business. My brother-in-law remained in the business for a while, supervising the handover.

Tudor house was our living accommodation whilst we were in business.

Olive Farthers is still in reasonably good health. November 1991.

Thomas Edward Franklin

I was born on the 10th February, 1904 at Gas Works Cottages which were at the end of present day Alne Close. Whilst I am known to most everyone, as Ben it was a name given to me by my school mates. I had four sisters and one brother. My father worked at the Gas Works and he also looked after the street lighting, switching them on and turning them off about half past ten at night. There were three gasometers. The coke from the ovens was sold to anyone who came along with a sack. They could have it filled for 6d. I can remember a wagon drawn by two horses and then there was another cart, just the one horse, both would be loaded each week with coke for Barrells Hall.

I went to school on the High Street between Milking Lane and School

'Fletcher's Ole which Ben never forgot.

Road. Our school headmaster was Mr. Robinson. One thing I can remember about him was the way he would go out into Milking Lane and cut a twig which he would use as a cane. He would give us so many handers, dependent on what we had been up to. Another of our teachers was a Miss Kirby. We would call her Flo. Kirby.

I was not very old when we moved to a cottage, one of four, which stood near by the mill (where Jasper Marsh is today) I believe the reason for the move was because my father had left the gas company and was now working for Mr. Joe Harris at Fosters Farm, Hall End. He went there as wagoner, and for ploughing, drilling and as a cowman. We moved from the cottage in the High Street to a cottage at Hall End which was much nearer my father's work.

Although I left school when I was eleven I was helping my father milking before this time. I never did seem to have much time for playing as other children did because I would get up at five o'clock in the morning to help my father with the milking. I would be in bed before seven o'clock in the evening.

Whilst I was at school I can remember an incident which I don't think I shall ever forget and that was a day during the summer. A number of us boys had gone to a spot just beyond the Mill which we called 'Fletchers Ole' it was just beyond the stank (small dam) and the river Alne. It was deep at this spot which allowed us to dive in. On this particular occasion we stayed longer than we should. Whilst we were in the water we noticed a man come along and pick up all our clothes and make off. We were all naked, we didn't have swimming shorts or anything like that. After a while we decided that there was nothing for it but to return to school. We decided that we would go back a way where we would not be likely to meet anyone, so we crossed the top of the High Street, made our way to the station and crossed the meadow (Brook End Drive) and came in the back way to school. We each had the cane for playing truant from school although we had no intention of staying away, we just lost track of time. We found out afterwards that it was the school's inspector, Mr. Lester who had collected all our clothes. One of the boys who had been swimming with us had decided to go back to school before us and had told the headmaster where we were. As children we had very little money to spend although I can remember Liquorice Allsorts, Blue Bird Toffees and Humbugs.

At home we used to feed pretty well.

Sunday: Roast Joint and Vegetables
Monday: Stew up of Sundays joint with vegetables
Tuesday: Pigs Chicklin & Veg
Wednesday: Rabbit Stew
Thursday: Roast Meat & Vegetable
Friday: Chicklins & Vegetables
Saturday: Make do
Afters: Jam Tart, Spotted Dog and Suet Duff.

Like a lot of other children we did depend upon clothes which were given to us. My mother would alter them if they did not fit us. Going out at five o'clock in the morning with my father during the winter, it used to be dark and cold, sometimes foggy. There was one time when my father and I climbed a style into a field, when it happened to be very foggy. When we came to leave the field we could not find the style, we walked round and round this field. My father always said it took us an hour and a half before we found that style. Our boss used to supply milk to all the houses in Henley and Wootton, he had a churn in a pony and trap. When I was fourteen I went to work for Mr. Cox at Hall End Farm as wagoner and cowman, like my father. I am not sure how long I stayed with Mr. Cox but then I went to work for Mr. Wright Jnr. at Botley Hill Farm. I still have a framed certificate which I was given whilst working for Mr. Wright. This is what it says:

Warwickshire County Council   Education Committee

Milk Competition

Certificate of Merit

This is to certify that at the time Mr. A. B. Wright was awarded a certificate of merit in the County Milk Competition 1934. Thomas E. Franklin was a regular milker in his employ.

Ben's father at the horses head outside the Black Swan, Henley-in-Arden. About 1880. Charles Washburn the Landlord.

During the time I worked for Mr. Wright I was loaned to his father when the mushroom season came round. We would pick mushrooms from early morning until we could hardly see. We were paid ½d. a pound and we earned some good money for those days. We would not be paid anything by the boss whilst picking mushrooms for his father but we were far better off picking mushrooms. These skips of mushrooms were loaded on carts and taken to Dansey Green Station where they went to the Birmingham market. It was good whilst the demand lasted but I don't know whether the demand went down but whatever happened slag was spread on these fields which killed the mushroom spoor. The fields were turned over to grass for grazing.

Round about 1935, I was still living with my parents. I got to know from a friend about a cottage in the High Street in Henley, that would shortly become vacant and would be 'to let'. My mother and father had often spoken of trying to move back to Henley. So I cycled off home, when I arrived my mother and father had gone to bed. To reach my bedroom I had to go through theirs. I noticed that my father was still awake so I told him my news. It turned out that this cottage, No. 41 High Street was where he had been born. We applied for the cottage and got it and here I still live after some forty three years.

Ben and the author by the open fire, sticks to the left of the range and logs on the right. Part of Bens wardrobe hanging up on the right. The blackened kettle is on top of the oven and a saucepan is on the left. Shovel hanging up behind Ben in case of an emergency.

I can't say when I went to work for a Mr. Parsons who was at Crockett's farm. In addition to his farming interests he was very interested in horses. He had stallions that would be taken out to various farms mainly in Worcestershire. He was also keen on Point-to-Point meetings which were very popular just before the second war.

I have travelled all over the place with horses, in those days we would go by rail. On one occasion I went with Mr. Parsons to a meeting at Dunchurch with a horse called Twank. This horse won his race quite easily. A chap came up to Mr. Parsons and offered 300 guineas for Twank, but the answer was "no". Another chap standing nearby said I'll top that offer by 50 guineas but still Mr. Parsons said no. He wanted to take him out hunting. About half an hour later I saw them coming back and noticed the horse was lame, we could not find out what could have caused this lameness. Mr. Parsons sent for Mr. Banham, the Vet at Stratford. He fired Twanks leg, I'm not certain what this did but it affected the veins. Poor Old Twank did not get better and I took him to the horse sales in London. I arrived there with Twank on the Friday night with another old horse. I could not get any lodgings so I stayed with the horses. On the Sunday morning I was reading a paper outside the stables when a car pulled up and who should get out but Percy Hawkes (butcher, Henley). He had come

Ben sitting in front of the window, which looked out on to the street, where he spent so much of the winter months watching the world go by. More of Ben's wardrobe hanging up behind the sofa, which he purchased from the local market for £15. Used a friends horse and cart to get it home.

down to London looking for a horse but did not find what he wanted. On the Monday poor Twank was sold for 60 guineas. We could not get a bid for the other horse which I had to bring back. I arrived at Leamington Station about midnight.

Whilst still with Mr. Parsons there was one night when he was going out to a big dinner and dance. One of our mares was expected to foal that night and Mr. Parsons asked me to stand by in case I could be of any help. About eleven o'clock I noticed the mare was in trouble so I went to the house and banged on the door. A window opened and one of the maids put her head out. I told her to phone Mr. Banham the Vet at once to come out. I think he only took eleven or twelve minutes to reach Crocketts Farm from Stratford. He turned to me after examining the mare and said 'that foals dead'. He asked if I could get any help to hold the mares head. I ran off to a neighbour who came back with me but not long afterwards he fainted. I went for someone else and blow me down if he did not faint. All this time Mr. Banham was cutting pieces off the foal to remove its dead body from the mare. About half-past two in came Mr. Parsons and without bothering to change his clothes he helped us to make the mare safe.

I then went to work for Fred Uzzle whose place was next to Yew Trees House. He was a builder and also the undertaker. I did general labouring and was also called on to dig graves at Wootton, Henley, Ullenhall and Oldberrow. I got 5/-d extra for digging a grave. A single grave was not too bad just five feet six inches deep but a double was seven feet six inches and the soil as you approached the bottom wanted a lot of throwing. You would shovel it to the edges then climb out and shovel away. I even dug two treble graves, they were nine feet deep. Of course you had to put up with all sorts of weather, there was no stopping just because it happened to be raining, the grave had to be ready for a certain day.

In Henley Churchyard half way up the slope there was once a ditch which ran across the width of the churchyard, people would throw old flowers and wreaths into this ditch. In the end they decided to fill it in and later on the ground was used for graves. I was called on to dig a number of graves where the ditch had been and those old wreaths certainly caused me some problems. I was all the time cutting wire and still the stuff would catch my arms so that they were covered in blood when I had finished. I can still remember whose grave I first dug where the ditch had been, it was a Miss Bryant from Liveridge Hill.

I cannot remember exactly when this happened but the policeman from Wootton would cycle up to Henley Police Station each day. On this one occasion he left his bike outside the station and went inside. When he came out the bike was gone. The very next morning a porter, I think it was George Pickford, came down from Henley Station with a bike on which there was a notice which said 'please deliver to Henley Police Station and let them know it got me safely to Birmingham.'

During the second war we had an 'Observer Corps' post on top of the Mount. A little job I had was to keep the place clean. I used to call at the gas works with a couple of buckets, fill them up with cold water, get a couple of red hot pieces of coke out of one of the ovens and drop a piece into each bucket. That's how I got my hot water.

The last seven or eight years of my working life I spent with the Warwickshire County Council, on the roads. It must be every bit of fifteen years ago that I had the last of my teeth out. Nineteen at one go. Dr. Farr gave me the gas. I had false teeth supplied. I tried them the once but have never bothered with them since.

I like a drink and have one everyday, more for the company. I do have drink in the house but never touch it, unless a mate comes to see me. I am quite happy here, I have my dog Jack, he's a great pal. I've had him for eight years. I have always had a dog but when Jack goes I don't think I'll have another one (died 1985), not at my time of life. I am hoping to see a few more Christmases. I always have a chicken for Christmas and perhaps I'll have a Mackie & Rum, my favourite drink.

I enjoy my garden, I grow most of the vegetables I require. My favourite flower which I grow every year is a 'Sweet Pea'. The soil in my garden is black and rich and I think this is due to the amount of human

soil which was dug in with ashes from the buckets which served as lavatories in sheds at the bottom of these gardens.
I never did marry.

Ben died in September, 1985.

Fred Harris

I was born on the 18th February, 1901 at 170 High Street, Henley-in-Arden. I had three brothers and three sisters. My father had a coal business, his depot was at the old station. I believe my father was born at Buckley Green. He went to the British School on the corner of Doctor's Row and the High Street (Brooklyn House). He had to pay 2d per week.

The school was used also as the Baptist Sunday School; this was before the school was built between Milking Lane and School Road. Mr. Bromborough was a teacher at the British School before he transferred to the Council School.

I attended St. John's Church for a number of years as a choirboy under the Reverend Bell. The choir was that large in those days that men and boys occupied all the choir stalls and the ladies got in the front two pews.

I can still remember some of the processional hymns we used to sing. 'Onward Christian Soldiers', 'Happy Band of Pilgrims' and 'Through the Night of Doubt and Sorrow'.

I can remember this vicar stopping his Sermon and apologising to the congregation if a choirboy misbehaved. He would come down from the pulpit, take the offending boy by the lobe of his ear, and march him off to the vestry, usually kneeing him in the bottom on the way. The boy would have to wait in the vestry until the end of the service before he received his punishment, usually a clip round the ear.

There was no payment to choirboys in my day, but once a year we would be taken on a days outing, possibly to Weston-Super-Mare, then perhaps a trip by boat down to Ilfracombe.

Sunday school outings were usually to Yarningale Common. My father would clean his coal cart down before the day of the trip, children would be seated on boxes and stools. Other tradesmen would help in transporting the children. Going up Blackford Hill the bigger children would be asked to get off and walk. Everyone thought it was a great treat. Flies were a problem for the horses so we used to pick May and Elder Blossom and wedge this in the horses bridle to help keep them off.

Tea urns were taken on the outings. Races were organised and prizes given to the winners. Coming home we would all sing songs. The High Street on a Sunday morning seemed to be full of people making their way to church or chapel. The bells of St. Johns and St. Nicholas would both be ringing at the same time, this was before they were united in 1915.

There was little for us children to do after school. We would go crow scaring to stop them picking up the seed. We would also collect wild flowers for our mothers to decorate window sills. We would go picking wild strawberries and blackberries which were made into jams and tarts.

In the autumn we would gather up fallen leaves which were used for the pigs bed, then later on they would be used on the garden. Scraps of everything would go into the swill tub or old milk churn. Some of the neighbours would give us odd scraps for the pig and when it was killed we would give them bits of the pig. The pig was killed by sticking and slitting the throat.

We played marbles with the clay and glass ones, then there would be a time when everyone was bringing out tops. We did tend to get into mischief on occasions for instance someone would get a pin and a button and a reel of cotton. We would then push the pin into the wooden frame of someone's window, and from the pin we would attach a button from a short piece of cotton which left the button lying against the window. Then a long length of cotton was attached to the button which enabled us to be at a safe distance, then we would keep pulling on the cotton which would cause the button to keep striking the glass. It was not long before the occupant would come out to see who was tapping at the window. Sometimes we were able to hide so that once the front door was closed we would repeat the performance much to the annoyance of the people in the house.

Another game was postmans knock. Our version was to blindfold one of our mates lead him to the front door of a house, then twist him round a number of times making certain that he finished up with his back to someone's front door. Then it was suggested that he kick backwards like a donkey. Of course there was a considerable crash and the occupants would come rushing out. Sometimes the offender would realise what he had done and run with the rest of us. If you should stand wondering what had happened then there was a chance that you might get caught and you could then get quite a whacking. You may wonder how we got anyone to agree to be blindfolded, we would promise that this game was something different to Postmans Knock, sometimes we were lucky in getting a victim.

We did from time to time have what they called a travelling theatre, I think the name of one of them at least was Holloways and Snape. They would put up a big tent somewhere and act various plays, mainly blood and thunder.

As young lads, if we had the money, we would take a trip from the old railway station, go to Lapworth, change, then take the train down to Hatton, change here and then get a train to Bearley. From here we would walk home, forget how long it took us. My father somehow raised enough money to buy a horse and trolley and start up a coal business. Father was quite a drinker. He worked from the wharf at old Henley station. I would think it was about 1910 I can remember giving him a hand to cart wood to the top of the Mount for a bonfire which was to be lit in celebration of King George Vs. coronation.

At 13 years of age I left school to work for my father for 5/-d a week. I did this for about two years then I joined a brother-in-law in London who was working as an electrician, in the Knightsbridge area. I did not stand this work for very long and got myself a job with a butcher, same area. One of the jobs I had was to go with a member of the staff to Smithfield Market to collect supplies of meat. We went by a cart drawn by two horses. We had to be back in the shop by six o'clock. I was not in this job for very long before I returned to my electrician brother-in-law. One of the jobs I did with him was to deliver petrol in cans to some of the big houses. We would store them in cabinets and bring back empty cans. This was before there were such things as garages as we know them. During the time I was doing this I saw King George V. and Lord Kitchener, not sure where they would be going. I also saw a Zeppelin fetched down by gun fire. This was towards the end of the first world war.

During this time I bought myself a suit and a bowler for 25/-. I also bought a watch for 2/- and a chain for 1/- — lost both items the same day via a pickpocket.

I have mentioned my father's drinking, there was a Mrs Harris who kept the Red Lion which was almost opposite to where he lived. When Sunday dinner was ready my mother would place a book in the front window and when Mrs Harris saw this she would not serve my father with any more drink.

There were a number of sick and dividend clubs run from the many pubs. These were the Foresters and the Oddfellows; the rules were strictly applied, if you went ill you were not allowed to be out during the period you were claiming benefit. At the end of the year there would be a share out of any funds remaining. If there had been a lot of illness during the year, then the share out did not amount to very much. Dividend clubs were mainly a way of saving for Christmas.

Saturday nights most pubs had a sing song that had the effect of attracting people in. I can remember Len Russell, retired policeman, who with his wife kept a small general store close to the Golden Cross (263 High Street) singing the following song, I can only remember one of the verses:

I love to see my dear old home again
that cottage in that little winding lane
I can see those roses climbing
I can hear those church bells chiming
and I'm longing for that dear old home again.

Author. Unfortunately Fred died before we had finished our chats.

Norman Beckwith Harris

I was born on the 20th November, 1902 at No. 83 High Street, Henley-in-Arden, the first son of my father's second marriage. He already had ten children and the eldest boy was serving in South Africa in the Boer War, when I was born. Three other sons had followed in their father's footsteps, he was a butcher and they each had their own shops before they were twenty one. My father had two children by his second wife. Before my mother married my father she had been a pianist and one of her engagements was playing for the 'Miss Beckwith Swimmers', a London group who performed tricks under water. One was smoking under water. It was never explained to me how this was done. It would appear that my Mother said to my father that if she ever had a son she would like his Christian name to be 'Beckwith', which is how I came by my uncommon name which in turn has resulted in my always being called 'Beck' Harris. My mother was a Londoner. I went to the school which is still standing, situated between Milking Lane and School Road, on the High Street. There were six class rooms as far as I can remember. Commencing with the infants then through to the age of 14 years, although some boys and girls would leave before this age. The classes were mixed. The head master was a Mr. Robinson. One of the teachers, a Miss Argyle, kept a paper shop next to the White Swan. There were private schools at Beaudesert Park, Arden House and Burman House. When I reached the age of ten my parents sent me to a commercial school at Stratford, situated in Greenhill Street, opposite the cinema (since demolished to make way for a super-market). I left this school when I was fourteen. During the winter months I travelled to school by train but in the summer months I used my cycle and thought nothing of it.

After school lessons whilst I was at Stratford I often assisted the drovers who were bringing cattle and sheep to Henley, some went on to Hockley Heath, Knowle and Solihull. It took us about three hours to get to Henley but we boys enjoyed helping. Some of the animals could not make the journey so we left them in fields at the side of the road and they would be collected by float the following day. The calves and other young animals would always be brought home by float. All my brothers were trained as I was to assist my father in his butchery business. Round about the age of 14 years I was assisting in the slaughtering of animals by the Pole Axing method. The humane killer gun was in operation but not compulsory until about 1930. Pole Axing sounds barberous by today's standards but you would not have been allowed to be a slaughterman unless you had proved your ability to do this job. Usually a halter was put on the animals head and a rope attached to the halter was passed through a ring in the wall and the animals head pulled down so that there was little or no movement. The area in which death results from a blow with an axe is fairly sizeable. I have known ladies approach us, willing to give us a humane killer gun rather than we use the Pole Axe. Cannot remember why we did not accept the offer.

I can remember setting off before five in the morning in the pony and trap for Birmingham meat market which we reached about six o'clock. There was a cafe there where you could buy a cup of coffee and rum for two pence. The memories still bring a warm glow. I am not sure when it was but my father started the Henley Market, distinct from the cattle market, which was operating once a fortnight on a Wednesday. My fathers market was at the rear of the Golden Cross and he dealt in Poultry, eggs and fruit. The farmers who brought their produce to be sold at the market would call on my father the following Friday morning after most of them had seen their milk on to the two minutes to eight train for Birmingham, to collect money due to them. There were about thirty or forty of these farmers and I could tell which farmer it was just by the trot or step of their pony. Most of the farmers who called would purchase their meat from my father. Eggs could be had 24 for a shilling. My father later moved his market to the Bear Public House, corner of High Street and Bear Lane but within a short while he moved to the rear of the White Swan. The reason for these moves was that the market was growing and there was insufficient space at either the Golden Cross or the Bear. The White Swan had the advantage of being close to Henley Station which was just across the meadow (now swallowed up by the Brook End Drive development). Talking of markets it was quite a sight to see some 200 cattle, sheep and pigs being driven from the Henley Cattle Market along the High Street to the old railway station which was where the present Abrasive Company have their factory and offices. There was always something to do for us children. A game we would play was to set a stone on top of a house brick then we would stand back and with other stones try and knock the stone off the brick. During the winter months we boys could often be found on the football pitch which was situated at that time between where Meadow Road now is and the river, kicking a football about by moonlight. Mind you we got into scrapes. I can remember a policeman catching hold of me for something, he clumped me round the ear then kicked my bottom and told me to tell my father what he had done. I never did tell my father but the policeman did with the result that my father gave me a whack for not telling him. An event to be looked forward to was the Horse and Flower Show which took place on the August Bank Holiday. The horse show was on the Monday and the Flower Show on the Tuesday. On the Monday there would be a parade of Shire horses, stallions, ponies, mares and their foals, hunters, dray transport tradesmen and their carts all newly painted, harness and hand rails highly polished and baskets displayed. There would be about twenty or thirty of these tradesmen competing.

It was a great pleasure to see some of the high stepping ponies drawing the traps. There was also jumping which reached a very high standard, in fact I would go so far as to say it was up to Olympic Class. It might not have appealed to townsfolk but for the country folk it was a great occasion. Anyone interested in horses had a great day because there were so many varieties being paraded. The show commenced at nine o'clock in the morning and would end about nine o'clock in the evening. There was a beer tent and a refreshment tent, everyone was catered for. One year we had a flood during the morning of the day fixed for the horse show. The water authority removed the stank (scots word for barrier) up by the mill where the owners had installed an engine to operate the grinding machinery, instead of relying on water power. Unfortunately nothing had been done to lower the stank at Blackford Mill, so the water in the river built up and overflowed over on to the show ground, which was to the west of the present Meadow Road. Somehow action was taken at Blackford Mill and the water was got away and the show went on.

Tuesday we had the flower show and also many sporting events in which school children and adults could take part. I used to enter for as many events as possible, including the mile race. Whilst I was reasonable successful in the events I entered, I never did win the mile. I came second many times to a chap named Hunt, he came from Earlswood, a good sport who trained specially for the half and the one mile races, whereas I did no training. I remember he worked for the Inland Revenue. There was the obstacle race, slow bike race, and pillow fight on pole placed across the river. There was also a greasy pole to be crossed. If you had any idea of entering these events you would need to wear a bathing costume. The fun came from those who fell into the river. There was cutting the ham down, whilst blind folded. You stood in front of the ham whilst they blindfolded you. You were then turned round three times and then it was up to you to find the ham, suspended between the two poles. Competitors would walk in all directions groping for the ham, which caused considerable amusement among the spectators. Prizes ranged from money to small gifts. The mile race was probably worth about 30/- to the winner, which was worth having in those days. There was never any shortage of entries for these events. All the surrounding villages would run similar events. Being a large family, whenever we had a party it was necessary to sometimes take over the shop or the area between the shop and our accommodation as a dining area using trestle tables. Four of my brothers were keen cyclists and I can remember three of them riding to London and back in a day. My brother Harold won a Birmingham to Weston-Super-Mare race.

Looking back we seemed to have far more snow during the winters than we do now. It seemed a regular pastime to be tobogganing down the slopes of the Mount. Another item which sticks in my mind is that at one time in Henley we had a Mr. North, Mr. South, Mr. East and Mr. West. Mr. West was the blacksmith who lived somewhere in the area where the present Midland Bank have their offices. Mr. East lived almost opposite. Mr. South lived in a cottage on the Stratford Road just beyond the playing fields. Mr. North lived in a cottage where Jasper Marsh now has his antique business.

Living next door to the place where I carry on my business (251 High Street) was a Mr. Roger Dare who sold wet fish from his pony and trap. In addition to his fish business the shop sold a few sweets. There was something which was hardly a sweet but was offered among the sweets, it was called 'Locust'. It was dark chocolate in colour, rather like a runner bean which had been dried and baked. It had pips inside at intervals, I suppose they were the seeds. It was of irregular shape, about an inch in width and a little over a quarter of an inch in thickness. The lengths varied from two to four inches. I cannot remember having ever seeing it since. Another sweet shop we enjoyed visiting, but which was mainly grocery , was called Dorrell's, which was where Lloyd's Bank now stands.

My Mother died in 1915. My father married again in 1923. My father was a choirister at St. John's for most of his life.

Like his father, Grandfather and Great Grandfather he was associated with the ancient Court Leet of Henley-in-Arden. All had been Town Criers. I in turn succeeded my father as Town Crier in 1923 handing over to my son Norman* in 1973 having completed fifty years as Town Crier. On the occasion of my retirement from this position I was presented by the Court Leet with a replica of the Town criers Bell. On it is inscribed

Adam Harris
Samuel Harris
Samuel Harris
Frederick W. Harris
Norman Beckwith Harris

The Manor and Township of
Henley-in-Arden
Presented to
Norman Beckwith Harris
on his retirement
by
The Lady of the Manor
To commemorate his 50 years as
Town Crier.

The duty of the Town Crier was to announce any special news items. We were quite busy before radio. We were well served for newspapers, the Birmingham Evening Mail would arrive on the 6.30 p.m. train from Birmingham.

Following my Fathers' death, the market he had started was transferred to Henley Auctions. His butchery business was sold to Gordon Masons father who had a poultry and fish business at King's Norton, Birmingham. I stayed with Mr. Mason for a year to assist him to get to know the Henley Trade. I still have a half sovereign which Mr. Mason gave me for some service I had rendered. Leaving Mr. Mason I joined Mr. H. Hawkes another butcher in Henley (116 High Street).

In 1925 I married a girl from Erdington, Birmingham. Whilst we were courting I used to cycle from Henley to Erdington which is quite a distance. In the same year as we were married we took over the Red Lion in Henley at a rent of 15/- per week. The previous tennant was a Miss Harris who had been at the Red Lion for 37 years. The public house belonged to Flowers Brewery. We naturally had to buy our beer from them but were permitted to purchase wines and spirits where we liked. The position is probably different today. We worked long hours, seven day a week but we were very happy. We had quite a good little business, doing a barrel of beer, 36 gallons and 2 × 18 gallon barrels a week. There were no pumps we used to draw the beer direct from the barrel. Saturday nights we would draw off in half gallon jugs just to save us too many trips up and down seven steps leading to the cellar. The pub had a boarded in bar and the regulars had their own seats. Woe betide anyone who should come in and sit down in one of these seats, until after the regulars had come and gone. These were the days of the depression, money was never plentiful. There always seemed to be kind people about who would provide soup to the needy. There were opportunities of earning a few shillings by holding a farmer's horse whilst he was in the market. You could also earn something by carrying a parcel from the market to say the station. Some people refer to those days as the bad old days but I have always thought of them as being good. Our business at the Red Lion was helped by stabling. We would charge a 1/- a day for a horse and we would have 20 or more on a market day.

In 1930 I left Mr. Hawkes to set up in the butchery trade on my own. I still occupy the same premises at 249/251 High Street. The premises had belonged to a Mr. Arnold who had a small shoe business. My heart has always been in the butchery trade, having been born into it. I no doubt had a good start but I have always worked hard to learn all I could about this trade. I pride myself that I have the knowledge to look at any animal and decide on the quality of meat it will produce. I can also by looking at cattle or sheep determine to within a pound or two what their dead weight will be. This is important to me as a retailer of meat. A number of farmers have wanted me to buy their animals at a fixed price but I have always insisted on paying them the current market price based on my estimate of the dead weight of the animal. I used to tell them if they doubted my judgement to come and see the beast slaughtered and then weighed. Not many took me up on the offer. I think they respected my knowledge. In the early days we relied on ice boxes to keep the meat fresh. I never had a great deal of trouble in this direction. I would ensure that there was a little moisture on the animals body after it had been slaughtered. I would keep it in as cool a place as possible, hang some cloths up soaked in vinegar to keep the flies away. Government inspectors visiting slaughter houses were very strict concerning hygiene and the quality of meat being offered for sale.

Weighing meat was done in the shop by the use of balance scales and using brass weights, many of which still stand in my living room window, which looks out on to the street. In 1933 we gave up the Red Lion, what with my butchery business and the fact that we were raising a family. We eventually had three boys and five girls, it was becoming too much for my wife.

After giving up the Red Lion I rented some 60 odd acres along the Redditch Road. It seemed the sensible thing to do. It complemented my butchery business by enabling me to keep and feed my animals. Later I increased to a 100 acres. At the outbreak of war I grew a small acreage of sprouts, potatoes, peas and mangolds. As farmers during the war we were required to plough up most of our land, although it was left to us which crops we grew. One year I grew an acre of flax at the suggestion of a ministry inspector which I subsequently sold to the government who had it sent to a special mill for processing.

I also looked after Mr. Masons butchery business whilst he was away in the Services. Meat was rationed in those days to 1/2d per week per person.

Since the War I have continued in my butchery business. Today (1977) I don't do so much as I used to. My son Jack has taken over the slaughtering and we have assistance in the shop. Even so I find a fair bit to do, with accounting and jobs that are necessary in a retail shop.

I am proud to sell quality meat and have many times purchased the prize winners at Christmas Cattle Shows at places such as Stratford, Warwick, Henley, Barnt Green and Bingley Hall (Birmingham).

Looking back I have enjoyed myself and would not have changed anything. I am glad to have been born when I was. I still regard the old days as some of my happiest.

Beck Harries died. October 1979.

*Norman died in 1986.

Marjorie Joyce Hawkes

I was born September 30th 1896 at 116 High Street, Henley-in-Arden, the same house in which my father was born and died in. I had three sisters and two brothers. My father carried on a butchery business which he took over from his father. My mother was Mary Jane Shakespeare who was born opposite to my fathers shop at 153 High Street. I understand that my mother's family could trace their ancestry back to William Shakespeare. My father has produced records going back to 1731. There was always lots of activity going on in our house. My father, in addition to his business, was involved with so many things happening in Henley, there were always people coming to see him for one reason or another. Opposite to us where

Mr. Harry Hawkes father of Marjorie and Percy.

Barclays Bank have their office was the Rectory which at the turn of the century was occupied by the Rev. Bell and his large family. They always had soup available for the needy, and my father would always be ready to supply some of the ingredients. My mother, although not a trained nurse, was frequently called upon to bandage bad cuts or give her opinion concerning a problem affecting the children, women seemed to prefer to discuss the matter with her rather than visit a doctor. It was just as well that my mother could undertake some form of surgery because she was often called upon to render first aid to some one in the shop who had either cut

The Stores (Mr. Godrich) now the site for Gateway's.

themselves or suffered from scalds. We used a considerable amount of boiling water, being butchers. The ground at the back of our premises was quite extensive and at one time stretched across to Fosters Farm at Hall End, that was before the railway was built. We had a considerable number of fruit trees, apples, gooseberry blackcurrants and plums. We used to have stacks of these in our cellars, we never seemed to sell any, apart from what we ate ourselves the rest were given away. Of course we would often receive something in return. For example I remember visiting Joe Steel for something and remarking on the wonderful mushrooms that were growing in a particular field. His answer was to help myself, he gave me a large round basket which I had no difficulty in filling and taking home. This was what happened. You never thought of selling such items, you helped one another. Of course most everyone grew vegetables and fruit of one sort or another.

I cannot remember there being a green-grocer in Henley until about 1910. I do remember a man coming to Henley from Birmingham with oranges when they were in season, he had a horse drawn cart and I can see my father holding his white apron open and this man would fill it with oranges for a 1/-. If he had not sold out by the time he reached the Golden Cross he would carry on to Wootton Wawen. Another travelling salesman came from Droitwich with a two wheeled horse drawn cart which was loaded with salt blocks about 24″ × 6″ × 6″. He called on all the butchers who used a fair quantity of salt for salting beef and rubbing into pork. Then there were

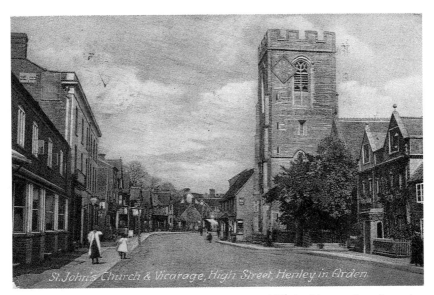

The scene that Mr. Fieldhouse and Mr. Hawkes would be looking at when discussing the future of the Guildhall (described by Marjorie Hawkes). The property on the right was the Vicarage now occupied by Barclays Bank plc. St. Johns Church has railings around the entrance. On the ground floor of the Guildhall were two shops, one a butchers and the other sold chinaware.

the bakers who used a fair amount. I know the man would always return to my father if he had not sold out, who would buy any unsold Salt at a slightly reduced price. I believe the reason for my fathers action was because he hated to think of the poor horse having to pull unsold salt back to Droitwich. My father was very fond of all horses and a very good judge. My brother Percy inherited the same love of horses and in my opinion knew as much about them as any vet. My father and brother John both served in the Warwickshire Yeomany, unfortunately my brother John was killed a few weeks before the Armistice was signed in November 1918.

On the subject of horses it was round about 1925 that my father attended a sale of cattle and horses, held at Leicester. He immediately took a liking to a horse which was on offer, whose name was 'Rob the Ranter'. My father's bid was successful and the horse duly arrived at our stables. My father visited many shows and made many purchases of horses, some of whom he would offer to friends and acquaintances who might want a hunter or a pony for one of the children.

One day my father received a visit from a Captain Paul who said he was looking for a horse for an elderly gentleman. He made a number of visits inspecting the horses, stressing that the gentleman was rather particular and that it was most important that the horse should be suitable for the person.

After a period of time my father and brother Percy were sorry to have ever become involved with this Captain. In the end the horse 'Rob the Ranter was finally purchased by Captain Paul. The gentleman on whose behalf 'Rab' was bought turned out to be King George V. For some reason which I don't know the King never did ride this horse.

I went to Burman House School which was a private school when I was five years of age. I think I was there until I was 12. The school was run by the three Miss Hawkins when I started. The French mistress could hardly speak a work of English. Later a Miss Martin took over. I remember she would go out to do some shopping and would say to us 'get your Bibles out and read them'. Once she was gone we would begin searching for the odd words that appear in this book and which somehow appeal to children because their meanings were not normally discussed in front of young people in my day.

Where Gateway Supermarket now stands was a small grocery shop run by Mr. Godrich. I know my father was able to help this gentleman's son, Victor, to find a suitable job after he had left school. Victor was later to have a hand in bringing the telephone to Henley, this was in 1909. He approached my father and said that providing there were ten subscribers to begin with the G.P.O. would consider it worth while to run the necessary lines. If memory serves me correctly Mr. Lodder was Henley 2 and we were Henley 7. We had far more public houses in Henley than we have today. Black Swan, Blue Bell and Three Tuns are still in existence. The King's Head at No. 70 High Street, The Bear where part of the present surgery is and the Old George opposite have gone. Further down the High Street almost opposite our shop was the Coach and Horses, now closed. The Nag's Head is still there and a little further South the Liquor Vaults. Just below our shop on the same side was the 'Old White Horse' 130 High Street. I remember the hanging flower baskets which Mr. Goddard, the landlord would water at seven o'clock every morning during the summer months. I almost forgot the Crossed Guns in Beaudesert Lane where the house "Riverside" now stands. The Red Lion and the Golden Cross still continue in business. The present 'off licence' at 169 High Street was the family home of the 'Coopers'. Wm. Cooper compiled the books entitled "The Records of Beaudesert", "Henley-in-Arden" and there was a book on Wootton Wawen.

My father was closely associated with St. Johns Church whilst my mother's family were 'Baptist'. On the subject of St. Johns I can remember attending a wedding as a bridesmaid and in my little basket I carried rose petals to sprinkle over the bride. This was before the days of confetti. I can also remember that the Organ needed something doing to it for which an appeal was organised. We at school were given cards which were divided into 12 squares. We had to try and get people to donate a penny and when they did they pierced one of the squares with a pin. When our card had twelve pin pricks we had to hand 12 pennies to our teacher.

Mr. Fieldhouse, who was closely associated with the Court Leet, was responsible for renovating St. Loos, High Street, which was originally three poor little cottages. His daughter Mrs. Barnard lived there for a short while. It was during the early part of the first World War that I can remember my father and Mr. Fieldhouse discussing the condition of the Guildhall which was in rather a poor state. I don't know what happened but Mr. Fieldhouse was responsible for having all the surface plaster removed and exposing the timber frame we see today. He was also responsible for carrying out repairs at Yew Trees and later had Austey Manor built for himself. This property is set back on the Stratford Road beyond Wootton Wawen and a little way beyond the Aquaduct. On a number of the properties he had dealings with he would have a small plaster cast of a Boar's Head let in to the brick work. I understand this was to commemorate the death of his son killed on safari by a boar. Mr. Fieldhouse died in 1928.

Marjorie Hawkes died in March 1985.

Verena Barbara Hemming

I was born at York House, 131 High Street, Henley-in-Arden in the year 1920. The name Verena was my father's choice, Barbara was my mother's.

My father was born at 81 High Street, and my mother at 107 High Street, Henley. She and her sister were dressmakers. During the first World War they sold from 107 a variety of grocery lines including Ice Cream.

My Great Grandmother kept the Windmill Inn at Little Alne, situated at the junction of the roads leading to Aston Cantlow and Great Alne, approached from Wootton Wawen. This would be about the beginning of the last century. In those days Inns would remain open all day. My mother told me two stories relating to the Inn, the first refers to a fight between a number of gypsies in the course of which a string of beads became broken and ended up all over the floor. My Great Grandmother gathered up these beads, which are quite unusual and had them made up into two strings, one of which was passed to my mother who gave them to me. Hardly a day passes without my wearing them. My father used to think they were made of some form of lava. The other story concerns a man who I think must have been a tramp, who went around with a bear on a chain lead. They would sleep rough for most of the year but in the very cold weather could be seen huddled up together under the bridge which carries the road to Aston Cantlow over the River Alne.

My father commenced his business of selling and repairing clocks and watches at York House* soon after the commencement of the present century.

Verena Hemming extreme left behind the little girl in a show called 'Calvacade of Song and Dance' given at the Memorial Hall in 1950.

This house has some interesting features, the shop front having a georgian window and I still have the shutters which protect the windows even to the glass in the door. Then on the second floor there is a grill let into the floor which allows light from a skylight in the roof to penetrate through to the landing on the first floor.

One of my earliest memories, I could only have been about three, was going with my father into the clock tower at St. Johns Church. He was responsible for winding the clock right up to the time of his death in 1955. I took over and carried on the winding of the clock until 1969 when my health forced me to give up. The actual winding used to take me about 45 minutes. One Sunday night I was locked in. There had been a Harvest Festival Service earlier in the day so I thought if I cannot get out I shall at least be alright for something to eat! I kept banging on the porch door, in the end I rang a bell to attract attention. Mr. Hodges who was responsible for locking the church was alerted by a Mr. Silman who was passing at the time and heard the banging.

The clock was made by Alexander Sadler Simmonds in 1868. He lived in Henley but his workshop was in Warwick. I am told that the clock face on St. Johns is identical to the one on the East Gate in Warwick.

My mother was educated at O'Connors, a small private school at Tudor

House in the High Street. I went to the school where most of the children in Henley went, between Milking Lane and School Road, I thought it was a very good school. When I was 14 I left this school but I had two further years of private education.

When I was young I walked a great deal with my mother. It was on one of these walks that I first became aware that I could sense where there had been tragedy. We were walking on Round Hill near Little Alne when I suddenly became very cold. I told my mother of my condition and we returned home. The next day we learned that a tramp had been found dead on Round Hill. I have had similar experiences of tragedy with no previous knowledge except this feeling which makes me aware that something unnatural had happened.

Both my mother and father had an inner sense of being able to fortell the future for people. I first began telling peoples fortunes when I was about 20 years of age. I still do it when requested.

My first job was at the telephone exchange in Henley, which was situated in the Stone House, by the Market Cross. I was 16 at the time and I stayed for 28 years, that was in 1964. The G.P.O. did present me with a certificate to mark this service.

When I was seven years I took the part of Zurika the Gypsy Maid in a production given by the Henley Operatic Society at the Public Hall. Father was a member of this Society.

After I had left school I took Singing and Elocution lessons. My teacher was a Madam Alice Vaughan who had been a pupil of Sir Henry Wood. Later on I used to teach the piano and give singing lessons.

These are some of the certificates I have received:-

1935. Leamington and County Competition Musical Festival. 'Girls Vocal Solo'

1938. First Class Award. Ladies Vocal Solo.
    Redditch Musical Festival Leamington Festival. Lieder Class Certificate
    Birmingham Music Festival. Certificate for Operatic Aria.

1946. First Class Award. Cheltenham Spa Annual Opera Competition

While all this was happening I took up ballroom dancing. My partner and I would cycle to village halls and visit the larger surrounding towns. Even went to the London School of Dancing. In some cases we gave exhibition dances. It will be quite obvious that I was leading a very full life and thoroughly enjoying myself. Dancing must have been in the blood because my grandmother and grandfather won a Blue Ribbon, a dance prize, at the Bull's Head, Wootton Wawen.

From 1935 until 1949 I was a teacher at the Sunday School. When I left I was presented with a Hymn Book A.M. (by Canon P. Webb.) which contains the musical accompaniment.

I still play my piano and sing to myself. Some of my sheet music is pre-second World War. In those days one of the Sunday newspapers would devote half of one of the inside pages to piano music in respect of the latest hit at that time.

I imagine that my father's family have been connected with Henley for about 400 years. I say this because this document which is dated 1668 and headed 'Indenture' refers to the transfer of a piece of land to John Hemming. My father was very much involved in all that went on in Henley. He was a member of the Court Leet. A member of the local Church Choir for 70 years. Leader of the bell ringers for many years. To mark someone's death on the day of the funeral, the Bell would be tolled 3 times for a man, 2 for a woman and 1 for a child.

Here I am unmarried and still living in the house in which I was born.

*131 High Street, Henley.

Mrs. Jessie Elizabeth Hobbins (nee Bayliss)

I was born on February 15th 1894 at 38 High Street, Henley-in-Arden, and youngest of eleven children, I had three sisters and seven brothers. I went to the Henley school on the High Street when I was three years of age. I was rather a weakling, I spent more time at home than I did at school. The school bell was rung as a reminder that we should be on our way to school. Before we went to our class-rooms we were lined up by class in the playground and we had to show our hands for teacher to see that they were clean. Our shoes were also inspected. During breaks we would play such games as hop skotch. Skipping if you had a rope, hoop, mainly wooden you would bowl it along striking it with stick. Sometimes at Christmas these hoops would be hung up and you would thread ivy and other greenery round the hoop which would act as a decoration. Not many people could afford to buy a Christmas tree. Whilst we all looked forward to Christmas we considered ourselves very fortunate to receive a small wooden doll with arms that moved. Then we had a small bag of sweets and some nuts. In the afternoon we would sit round the fire hearth and sing carols. We were most happy. We always received a ½d. pocket money on a Saturday and it was never too early for us to be asking our father for our pocket money. We would mainly spend our half-penny at Badgers the bakers and sweet shop which was where Beechcroft now stands. Our favourite sweets were dolly mixtures, jelly babies and you could get a toffee on a stick for a ¼d.

We did not have any holidays but once a year our Mother would take us

The shop where Mrs. Hobbins and her brothers and sisters spent their ½d. In those days the shop belonged to Mr. Badger and stood where the present Beechcroft Development stands.

into Birmingham by Carrier Cart, where she would do some shopping. We looked on this trip as our annual holiday. We did go for a Sunday School outing, this was usually to the farm where Haven Pastures on the Birmingham Road now stands. We played games and had races and thoroughly enjoyed ourselves. If it should be raining we played in the cow shed. We were usually given an orange to come home with. There used to be coaches drawn by horses which came from Birmingham which would be taking a party of people perhaps to Stratford, they would stop in Henley for an hour or two whilst the people went for something to eat and drink. Some of the poorer children would black their faces and run alongside the coaches as they entered Henley, asking for money. The passengers would throw out coppers which would be scrambled for and especially if they had drunk too much they would even throw out silver. I can even remember some saying 'there goes the rent money'. My mother would warn us against begging for money. Whilst the party were taking their refreshments the coaches would stand in Doctors yard, where the rehabilitation centre now stands. As children we loved to clamber up and sit in these coaches whilst they were unattended.

On a Saturday evening just before Mr. Harris the butcher closed he would auction any offal that he had not sold. Sausages, liver and tripe would be offered on a plate with a request 'who'll give me 3d. for this,' dependant on what was on the plate. We children would rush down to meet our mother and ask 'what have you got mum'. We always enjoyed Saturday's tea.

Beaudesert Lane has changed quite a lot over the years although the Parish Room is still the same as I remember it, a rather poor area. I remember also one couple in particular where the man, when he had had too much to drink would knock his wife about and she would be badly bruised. The police would come and take him to the police station and lock him up. Yet the next day the woman could be seen making her way up the lane on her way to the Police Station with her husbands breakfast or dinner. There was another rather poor area to the left of the Blue Bell Inn, called the Tan Yard which had about 6/7 cottages which only had a front door and a small piece of garden in front. At the rear of the yard there were two steps which led to the river where some women would do their washing using rubbing boards. There were a good number of tramps about when I was a child. There was a lodging house for them at what was then Chingley Bank where the present De-Montfort Court is. The cost of staying there for these tramps was 1/- per night although I believe they could obtain a voucher from an office which would entitle them to one night's lodging. These tramps would often knock at our door asking for hot water and presenting dirty old cans, and then ask for a little tea and had you any old shoes or clothing. Where Henley Garages now stands stood Ashby House where Miss Cook lived. She had beautiful gardens at the rear, ornamental ponds with gold fish. She had two dogs, one very small which she called 'Spider'. It looked like one. The other was a St. Bernards, when it died she had it stuffed and it used to lie in front of the fire place in the living room. She was however a very mean person, she would give children a rotten apple to run an errand until they got wise then they would run past her house. Miss Cook visited my parents once a week to play cards. I think they played whist. Part way through the evening she would take from one of her pockets a piece of swede to eat. My mother visited her occasionally and would always take some cake or buns which she hid under her apron. These were for Miss Cook's maid who had a very hard life. I understand Miss Cook owned a number of farms which were rented out. One thing Miss Cook was good at was what we called poker work. I never actually saw her doing this but I understand she had a fine poker which she got red hot and then would burn a picture on to wood, I have seen some of the work, horses and dogs, they were beautiful. When I was married she gave me a cameo brooch.

At the rear of our cottage we had a water pump. Our toilet which was at the end of the garden was a double seater, one for the children and the other for adults. Lighting was by oil lamp. We purchased the oil from a man who came round with a barrel on his cart. We purchased a pint or perhaps half a gallon depending on what money was available. Englands Glory Matches were 1½d a dozen boxes. On the floor of the cottage we had lino. We also

Miss Annie Cook referred to by Mrs. Hobbins with her two dogs in her garden.
There was a novel written by Keble Howard (pen name) son of a Henley Rector,
George Edward Bell (1876-1915) based on this lady and her garden called 'The God
in the Garden'.

had rag mats which consisted of usually sacking material for the back and
thin strips of all sorts of material which were somehow sowed through the
sacking. My father would have a pig and about a dozen hens and would
grow most of the vegetables we required. My mother would buy a rabbit
from time to time to bring some variety to our dinners. She would always
have vegetable soup available, it was that thick you could stand a spoon up
in it. My father went to work on a three wheel cycle and if he was in a good
mood he would give us a short ride standing on the back. He worked at
Barrells Hall as did one of my brothers and two sisters. Their employer was
Squire Newton. I attended Evening Classes where you could take lessons in
Arithmetic, spelling, cooking and sewing. These were to help us when we
left school to find a job. Usually most girls went into Service. I remember
Muriel Johnson (Johnsons Transport, Henley) making a beautiful 'Side
Board' they had wood-work classes for girls as well as boys. One night when
I was returning from these classes, as we approached the White Swan it was
clear from the number of people standing around that something had
happened. It appeared that the fire-engine had been called out which was
drawn by two horses. The driver was a Mr.Jackson who, attempting to pull
up by St. Johns Church to pick up the Sergeant, had pitched forward and
was thrown on to the road. He apparently had broken his neck and died
almost immediately. He was carried into the White Swan because the law at

that time was that anyone who died accidentaly should be taken to the nearest public place to where the accident occurred. There was, about the same time, the body of a man found in the river just beyond the Mill. He was taken into the Black Swan. I presume to await the arrival of a Coroner. On the night of the accident to Mr. Jackson there was 'olde time dancing' taking place at the White Swan, this was a weekly event, this was stopped and the rest of the programme cancelled.

When I was fourteen I left school, the day was a Friday. The very next day Saturday I was off to Liverpool with a friend to take up a job in service. My Mother obtained the position for us by answering an advert, I believe it was in the Stratford Herald. The gentleman I worked for was I understand a nephew of Mr. Gladstone. There were fifteen servants and we were paid quarterly by a secretary and required to sign a receipt. On Sundays we had to go to Church and we would stand outside until our employer had entered. He would look at each one of us just to ensure that we were all present. After the Service we would hurry off back to the house to change into our livery and continue with our work. Whilst our employer was strict he was very good to all the servants. During the shooting season he would always see that our parents received either a brace of pheasants or something similar, perhaps grouse. At Christmastime our parents always received a lovely hamper. I stayed at Liverpool for about two years. I had two or three jobs following my return from Liverpool. I worked for a short while as kitchen maid for Doctor Nelson at Arden House School. I also worked for Mr. Arthur Mitchell of Mitchell and Butlers the Smethwick Brewery Company. Mr. Mitchell had taken over the vicarage at Leek Wootton, near Kenilworth. The house was too large for the vicar and he lived in a smaller house close by. I then joined Mrs. Docker at Kenilworth whose son Bernard was later knighted and became Chairman of B.S.A. I remember that both Mrs. Docker and Bernard worked very hard during the first World War, knitting socks, and other items for the troops. Four of my brothers served in the first World War and all came back safely. I lost a son in the Second World War, killed on the beaches of Normandy.

I married in 1918 in St. John's Church, Henley-in-Arden. My husband had been given seven days leave from France. I went to my wedding in a horse drawn cab which came from Hockley Heath. There were no motor cars or cabs available in Henley at the time. My husband had served an apprenticeship as a carpenter before the War with a company in Coventry. After he was demobbed he returned to his job and we lived in Coventry for a short while, until a cottage became available for us in Henley, this was next door to the 'Elms' where beechcroft now stands. The cottage consisted of two rooms upstairs and a small attic. The kitchen you could hardly get two people in it. Off the kitchen leading to the back door was the store for coal, very small. Six of my children were born in this cottage. Washing day took up all of Monday. I used to have a woman come in and help me on this day, I paid her 6d. Neighbours would come and ask for a bucketful of suds.

We would sometimes put their whites in with ours. We used to soak all the clothes before putting them into the copper. Swilled them in clean water, blue them to keep them white. There was much more neighbourliness in those days. The copper provided hot water for the bath, in those days an iron one. We also used the copper to boil the pigs swill. My husband had two allotments along the Ullenhall Road just past the railway bridge on the right. On nice evenings he would say 'come on Mother get the children ready and lets go to the allotments'. This little outing caused great excitement. After a few years my husband began to breed pigs and sell them to local butchers, this helped our income. On one occasion we lost a sow who was due to farrow when she developed swine fever and had to be destroyed. When she was opened up it was found that she would have produced 15 babies. We were however helped by the kindness of a Mr. Baxter (Marsh & Baxter) who lived along the Birmingham Road. When he heard of our loss he had a collection amongst the butchers and farmers and with the money we were able to purchase another pig. Many's the time when a sow has produced more pigs than she could feed that my husband and I would take the excess pigs away and feed them with a bottle in front of the fire at intervals of two hours. We would take it in turns throughout the night. They used to have what they called a 'pig club' which used to meet in the Red Lion, in Henley.

Bringing up a family was not easy but we managed and were very happy. In 1929 we moved into a new house in School Road provided by the Council, where the last two of my family were born. The rent was 6/6d per week. We had a bath room which was a real treat. Some two years later electricity was installed and our rent was increased by 6d per week. Opposite our house was the school meadow. This was divided into small plots and children were encouraged to cultivate the ground as part of their education. The produce they grew was sold mainly to their parents and the proceeds helped to buy new seed. We had some wonderful Carnivals between the Wars. I cannot remember where they started but they processed along the High Street to Beaudesert Park where games and races were arranged. We looked forward each year to the arrival of the Mop. There was a Pig or Ox Roast. Mr. Fieldhouse, Lord of the Manor, who did a lot for Henley, was very good in that he saw to it that slices of meat were sent to the poorer families. When anyone died neighbours would always draw their curtains on the day of the funeral. The Church Bell would toll — one for each of the persons life. When a funeral left a house the front door was never locked until after the mourners had returned. I do not know the reason for this.

My family have grown up and I am fortunate in that they live in and around Henley and I see them every week.

Mrs. Hobbins died in October, 1985.

Marjorie Hodges, Nee Edkins

My paternal grandfather J. Edkins came from Gypsy Hall Farm, Wilmcote and with my grandmother moved into Brooklyn House, 46 High Street, Henley-in-Arden. My maternal grandmother, who had been widowed, came from Dunstable with my mother in 1888 and took over the 3 Tuns Public House at 103 High Street, Henley. My mother married Walter Edkins from Brooklyn House in 1905. I was born the following year. My mother and father set up house at 5 Alcester Road, Stratford-upon-Avon. They made one or two moves and eventually came back to, I think, number two Alcester Road, Stratford, where my father died in October 1918 of the flue epidemic which raged at that time. My mother then decided to move to Henley and join her mother at the 3 Tuns. My grandmother died in 1919 and my mother took over the public house. In 1921 or 22 she sold the house to Holts Brewery of Birmingham, but remained as tenant manager until 1929. My grandparents at Brooklyn house had found living on the High Street not to their taste and had moved to The Meadows at Buckley Green. One of my memories from my 3 Tuns days was that on each New Year's evening, Tommy O'Donnell would sing.

"The Miner's Dream of Home"

I cannot remember why he should choose this occasion to sing that particular ballard, I cannot even remember how long it went on for. I used to attend the Sunday School which in those days was held at No. 47 High Street, now occupied by Brookhouse Insurance. The outside of the property has hardly changed but I cannot say what changes have been made to the interior. In 1925 I joined the Henley Amateur Operatic Society, we used the public hall for our shows. I could sing fairly well and play the piano. I can remember an occasion, it was sometime during 1927 when we took one of our plays to Earlswood. In this play a number of the male cast were required to wear helmets. The obvious thing was to approach members of the local volunteer fire brigade who readily agreed to loan their helmets. Of course the inevitable happened, there was a fire and four or five firemen reported for duty without helmets. I cannot remember what the outcome was.

I first got to know Osborne Hodges through his coming into the 3 Tuns on Saturday evenings with other members of the Henley football team. He only drank shandy. It was a few weeks before Christmas 1923 that he asked his sister Babs to ask me if I would come to a party his family were having at Christmas, he was too shy to ask me himself.

One of my fondest memories during the time we were courting was a Sunday evening just before Christmas, I think the year was 1927. We had been to Evensong at St. John's and we were walking down the High Street. The night was cold and there was a frost, the moon was full out and the stars sparkled in the sky. We turned left at the Golden Cross and walked to the top of Blackford Hill. There was complete silence except for the bells of St. John's which were ringing for Christmas, a custom practiced in those days. It was a memorable occasion for me which I shall never forget.

Another memory from my courting days concerns Good Friday. On this day Osborne's mother together with his brother and sisters and myself would set off to visit a friend of Osborne's mother, Mary Peace who lived at Kates Cotage, Kyte Green. We would take quite a supply of Hot Cross Buns. We would set off down Beaudesert Lane, go over the Mount until we reached Edge Lane. We would turn left and soon come to Kates Cottage. This went on for quite a number of years but I cannot think why and when we stopped going. I never remember the weather interfering with our journey.

I was married to Osborne Hodges in 1929, the year that my mother gave up the tenancy at the 3 Tuns. We were married in St. John's Church and the reception was held in the Assembly Rooms at the back of Welch's bakery (still the bakers shop in Henley but under different management). Our first home was at No. 9 School Road which we moved to in 1929 and which was a new council development. My mother had been fortunate enough to secure the house at No. 7 School Road she died in 1934.

Authors note.
I became acquainted with Marjorie and Osborne soon after I came to Henley in 1964. One of my great interests in life has been railways, particularly steam. My wife happened to mention this interest during the course of a conversation with Michael Hawkes, butcher, who suggested that I should visit Osborne Hodges who had a very fine model railway layout. Michael had not exaggerated. It was situated in a shed in the garden and I would estimate that the layout measured approx. 12 feet by seven feet. There were two or three main tracks circling the layout. There were all sorts of model engines, carriages and goods trucks by the dozen. There were stations with model people and most of the things you would have seen on a railway station before the second World War. Roads flanking the tracks had model houses and shops in the appropriate places, tunnels, signals all connected to control boxes which in turn controlled the movement of all the rolling stock. Osborne was a meticulous person over this layout. Not so long after our first meeting we formed a small model railway club, which flourished for quite a few years. At first we worked in some outbuildings at the back of Michael Hawkes butchers shop. Later we purchased a wooden hut which is still standing on the Sports and Social Clubs ground. For quite a few years we would produce a railway layout for display on Carnival Day.

Unfortunately Osborne's health declined and he subsequently died in August 1977. I have maintained contact with Marjorie and we enjoy a chat mostly about old Henley.

Although Osborne told me a number of stories concerning his early days I never actually made any notes except for one which always struck me as funny but not for the participants. It concerns the local fire brigade during the early thirties. They received a call one winter's evening from Lowsonford, not only was it dark but it was also foggy. The Engine set out with Osborne walking in front waving a handkerchief to act as a guide for the driver. They eventually reached Lowsonford but there was no sign of any fire. Osborne decided to knock on a cottage door to ask for information. The occupant thought for a moment after answering the door and then remembered there had been a fire but it had been out for some time. I cannot remember whether Osborne ever told me how the fire men reacted or what time they arrived back in Henley.

Roy Johnson

I was born at No. 71 High Street, Henley-in-Arden, on the 15th February 1913, the youngest of four; I had two brothers and a sister. My mother was a Horsley from Wootton Wawen, a very old established family in those parts. There is a gravestone in Wootton churchyard to a Horsley dated 1600, just cannot remember the exact date. My mother's mother came from Long Compton, she was a Mary Anne Hibbard, one of twelve children, but only six survived. My mother died in 1969, she was 92 years of age. She left school when she was eleven (1888). The first school she attended was at the Parish Room in Beaudesert Lane. She has told me how she would run errands for John Hannett, the author of a journey through parts of the Arden countryside, published sometime during the 1860s. He was High Bailiff from 1873 until 1893, and lived at the Gables on the High Street. My father's family came from Birmingham. He came to Henley after a row with his father. His first job was a coachman to a family living at Beaudesert Park. He later went into business on his own account as a carrier travelling mainly between Henley and Birmingham. One of my earliest memories is standing on the door-step with my mother listening for the horse-steps of my father's horse returning from Birmingham. Another memory of about this time was hearing the peculiar sound of the engines from a Zeppelin probably on its way to Birmingham. Although I was quite young I associated them with fear. I have another memory round about this time it concerned a trip which my mother made with my father on most Thursdays to purchase groceries for our little shop (Station Stores). After my mother and father had left, my grandmother would give me two pennies to buy three or four eggs from Mr. Coppage who kept hens at the back of his workshop which was where Torquil Pottery is now, he was a builder and carpenter and I know he also made coffins as well. With these eggs my grandmother would make us pancakes — this went on for quite a while.

Fathers first Motor Bus.

During the early part of the twenties we moved to our present address, 32 High Street, which at that time was known as Lythian Place; and where my Uncle had carried on a small cycle and car repair business. He was also able to repair guns. My parents bought the business and property from him.

In 1924 my father purchased his first motor bus, I can remember going with him to a place in Moseley, Birmingham to collect it. The cost was £1,000 which was a lot of money in those days. It could be converted from carrying passengers to goods. You can see from the photograph it had a tail board at the rear and also a ladder at the rear which enabled you to climb up and stack goods on the roof.

As young children many of our games were based on the war that had just ended; we played on the ground where Cherry Orchard is. We even attempted to dig trenches. If you were unfortunate you ended up being a German.

Sometime after the first world war a German field gun appeared on the bowling green at the back of the White Swan, I have no idea where it came from or what happened to it.

My mother has told me that when she was a child No. 38 High Street was used as a Quaker meeting house. Many of the people attending would arrive on horseback; some before they went in would put a nose bag on the horse. When the meeting was over and the people had departed my mother and some of her brothers and sisters would be told by their mother to go and sweep up the chaf which had been dropped by the horses. This was fed to the fowl, not much wasted in those days.

I went to the council school with my brothers and sister. The Head Master in my time was Mr. Walker who with the other teachers were great disciplinarians so far as reading, writing and arithmetic were concerned. I can remember feeling very jealous of those boys and girls who could read better than I could, of course I am speaking about my early days at school. Later on I was one of three boys to win the first scholarships awarded at our school. I would be between 10/11 years of age. I went from Henley school to Solihull School where I remained until I was 17.

I went from Solihull to Saltley College and remained there for two years on a teacher training course. My first teaching appointment was at a school in Smethwick. My sister Muriel was also teaching in Smethwick but not at the same school as I was. We travelled together by train from Henley to Moor Street, then we would go across to Victoria Square and catch a tram which travelled from the north side of the square down to the parade then Dudley Road and straight on into Smethwick. During the thirties Henley had a rat catchers club and for a time I was fixture secretary, that meant I would arrange with farmers locally what date, usually a Sunday morning, between ten and twelve o'clock, it would be convenient for us to pay a visit with our dogs. There was one farm where we accounted for over 400 rats in a morning, the poor old dogs were exhausted and members were killing rats with sticks. I can remember we went to the local pub and we put paid to 89 pints of beer. There were ten or eleven of us. I also remember saying ro the landlord what about some bread and cheese but he refused. It was customary for landlords to supply the club members with free bread and cheese because we had quite a following and it meant some useful trade to him. We let him know we should not be returning to his house again.

At the outbreak of the Second World war my mother decided to bury her best china somewhere in the garden. After the war no one could remember where she had buried this china. After much digging we found it below the chicken run.

Frederick G. Maine

My Grandfather on my father's side was born on a ship coming to England from America. I have no idea why the family was coming to England, all I know is that he married a lady from Moreton Morrell. My father was born in Stratford-on-Avon in 1885 the same year as my mother. I was born at No. 1. Beaudesert Lane, Henley-in-Arden in 1908, one of five children.

The cart I helped to pull with the rope round my middle when going up hill. In the background my father sister Nellie, mother holding another sister and my brother George sitting on the doorstep.

Our Donkey with me on its back.

Our horse and cart outside No. 1. Beaudesert Lane. With my mother at the horses head and my sister Nellie with hands on my shoulders.

Both my grandfather and father were chimney sweeps. I have also swept chimneys from time to time.

I cannot be sure of the year but it would be somewhere just before the beginning of the first World War that my father opened a little green-grocery business at the house where we lived. Apart from selling from the house he had a small hand cart which he loaded with fruit and vegetables and not only called on houses in Henley but he would visit the surrounding villages. When I was not at school I would go out with my father on his greengrocery round. Before we went up a hill he would tie a piece of rope round my middle with the other end attached to the cart. We would set off with me pulling as hard as I could, I would only be about eight years of age, and my father pushing the cart. I have often wondered how worthwhile it was taking into account the miles we trudged and the amount we sold. Some of the people we served were not always able to afford what they had ordered and my father would say 'leave it to next time'. When we did call again and asked for our money there were some who would say it was less than what we said. My father was not a great business man, he would not argue but accept what he was given. My mother would also take out vegetables and fruit on her bike. Chimney sweeping was my fathers main business, he sold vegetables when he was not sweeping. Another little sideline was selling newspapers. He would go to Henley station to meet the Birmingham train with the evening newspapers. Collect his Evening Despatches and hurry off down Station Road to the High Street where he would call out 'papers'. He would also visit all the pubs. On Saturday evenings he would also have the Sports Argus in addition to the Despatch. There was competition from Dalby's who sold the Birmingham Mail. I commenced school in the High Street when I was three and left when I was fourteen.

Our business must have improved because my father first bought a donkey to help him in the greengrocery business then he bought a horse and a cart, which enabled him to carry more fruit and vegetables on his rounds.

Although we would look forward to Christmas it was not a time of plenty. My father would cut from a hedge part of a holly tree and that would be our Christmas tree. In our stockings we would have a few new pennies, an apple and orange and some sweets.

There were times when I would go out with my Grandfather when he was not sweeping chimneys. We would walk miles calling at cottages to see whether they had any rabbit skins to sell. You always went round the back and you could tell because the skins would be nailed to a door for drying. My Grandfather would offer a penny a skin or two pence if the head and legs were attached. He would then sell these skins in the Birmingham market for six pence to eight pence each skin.

On the corner of Station Road opposite the police station was the Filbert Cafe which had a filbert tree in the garden. If we should be going by on my fathers horse and cart I would grab a handful of nuts, in the season of course.

Although my father enlisted at the outbreak of the Great War he was invalided out very soon afterwards. What my father has left from that time are six diaries, each one consists of about eight school exercise books. He was not a well educated man by any means but, using pen and ink he has recorded almost a daily entry of happenings during the years of this war. Many entries are newspaper cuttings and pictures, other items are based on things he either read or was told.

Here are just a few entries taken from the first diary.

July 11th, 1914   Fish famine commences. Plaice 24/- for 14 lbs. Cod 11/3d for 14 lbs. Hake 9/- for 14 lbs. Lemon Soles 19/6d for 14 lbs. Dover Soles 3/- a lb. Fresh Herrings and Bloaters 16/- for 100. Haddock 9/9d for 14 lbs. Kippers 6/- − 7/- for 30 pairs. Lobsters 20/- − 60/d for 20. Crabs 38/- per hamper. Hallibut 18/3d for 14 lbs.

Jan 29th, 1915   Coal 1/4d per cwt. or 26/- − 31/- per ton. Bread 7½d per 4 lb loaf. Cheese 11d per lb. Beef Mutton Pork advance a 1d per lb. Pork from 7½d to 1/- per lb. Mutton 6½d to 1/1d per lb. Beef from 7d to 1/3d a lb. Potatoes 1d a lb. Onions 2d per lb. King Edward Potatoes £5.5.0d a ton.

Feb 3rd, 1915	Announcement by Chief Constable of Warwick County, Mr. John Brinkley. In case of Air Craft Raid, first for people to get in the cellars and keep in the houses. Second for people to doubt the lights and keep them out all night. The warning will be given by siren or hooter or Church Bells. In the case of Henley-in-Arden notice will if possible be given by the ringing of two Church Bells by Mr. Harry Hodges of 110 High Street.
Feb 11th, 1915	Police of Birmingham would like to hear of any airship that has been seen about Birmingham.
Feb 22nd, 1915	Cheese 1/3d per lb.
Mar 24th, 1915	Suspension of train services to Lapworth from Henley-in-Arden.
Apr 9th, 1915	Mr. Andrew Walker inventor of Bovril died today aged 78 years.
Apr 10th, 1915	Birmingham Market. Green vegetables make famine prices. Cabbage cuttings, usual price 9d per beg todays price 2/-. Curly Greens 1/6d now 3/-. Cheshire cabbage made 6/- a pot.

After the war we had film shows at the Public Hall (Memorial Hall) the operator came from Moreton-in-Marsh. He would advertise his arrival by sounding a four note horn fitted on his car.

During the interval the operator would show a few advertising slides. My father had one in connection with his chimney sweeping business.

After leaving school I helped my father for two or three years but as there was not much work in Henley I decided to join the Army.

Harold Edward O'Donnell

I was born on the 9th November, 1902 in a small cottage behind where De-Montfort Court now stands. I had six sisters and two brothers. My mother died when I was quite young, my father was a blacksmith working for a Mr. Morris. The forge was almost opposite to the Yew Trees House on the High Street. He worked there for many years shoeing and repairing farm implements. The wages were not very great even for those days, 18/- per week. In the end my father had to give up the work due to failing eye sight. For the rest of his working life he took any job he could get on local farms. He has even walked to Redditch in search of work as he could not afford a bike.

I started school when I was five walking to the R.C. School at Wootton Wawen which consisted of two classes, one for the infants, five – seven years, then we went into the senior class. The teachers did their best to teach us English, arithmetic, history, geography, dictation, singing and we had drill which they now call P.T. Our school was joined to the Mill at Wootton. It was a two story building, the teachers lived on the ground floor and our class rooms were upstairs. Walking as we did from Henley, if it was raining we would arrive soaked. The teachers were very good, they always seemed to have some dry clothes and they would make us change. We were not always given boys clothes to change into but the other children knew better than to laugh at us.

My young brother Frank had bad feet and to get him to school one of my sisters and I used to push him to Wootton in a little home made wooden trolley. Another thing we did going to and from school was to look for ladies hair-pins, the one who found the most was the winner. Despite the fact that we were very poor we somehow always seemed to enjoy ourselves. Local people were very good to us. The White House in the High Street was owned by a Mr. & Mrs. Cooper, often as you went by they would tap on the window and we would go to the door where we would often be given clothes or boots which my father was very grateful for. About a week before Christmas my father would tell us to go and sing a carol to each of the people who had been good to us throughout the year, but we were not to take any money. Father said that this would show our thanks for what they had done for us. Also about this time all the boys and girls from school would go across to the 'priory' a big house opposite to our school which was occupied by Mr. & Mrs. Fieldhouse and sing carols. Mr. Fieldhouse would give each of us twelve new pennies, they were dated for the coming new year. This gift was a small fortune to us children. I was never allowed to keep the money but handed it over to my father who did have great difficulty in supporting us. We would also go to Wootton Hall where Mr. Hughes lived and sing carols. We would come away with a bag of goodies, orange, apple and nuts. Mr. Hughes would also arrange for each boy to receive a pair of short corduroy trousers and the girls would receive material sufficient to make a frock. Mr. Guiness who followed Mr. Hughes at Wootton Hall carried on with these gifts. These gifts were also made available to the children at the Church of England School on School Hill close to Mayswood Road. Whilst we were at the Hall we would be shown Magic Lantern Slides which were really magic to us children.

There was a Mr. & Mrs. Coates who lived in a cottage where De-Montfort Court now stands, they used to be so pleased when on Palm Sunday we children would take them a bunch of real Palm, we really got a thrill out of seeing these people being so pleased with our gift.

In our playground at school stood a pole from which hung about six double lengths of chain. You would get yourself inside one of the double chains, other boys doing the same then all run the same way and it would act as a swing, once you took your feet off the ground. We had a game which we called 'tip cat'. You had a short piece of wood about four or five inches in length, sharpened to a point each end which you placed on the ground. Each boy would have a stick, the idea was to strike one end of the wood on the ground which caused it to spin into the air, you then attempted to hit it as far as you could. You had three chances, if you failed to strike the small piece of wood you were out. The winner was the one who had struck the small piece of wood the farthest. We measured the distance by paces. We played marbles, these were the coloured clay type. We played hits and spans — you attempted to hit the other boys marble. You would normally play in the curb. The span came in when you got your marble close enough to the other boys marble that you could by using thumb and little finger touch both marbles, and if you could you took your opponents marble. Some boys would have a piece of wood which could be stood up and which had five or six openings cut into the edge that stood on the floor. Over the openings was a number, the smaller the opening the bigger the number, say five or six, the larger holes would only be worth say one or two. The object was to bowl at these openings, if you were lucky enough to get one of your marbles through you would be given the number shown over the opening. Any that did not go through were kept by the boy who owned the wood with the openings cut into it. There were games to be played with cigarette picture cards. One of these was for three of us boys to each stand two or three cards up against a wall then you would each stand on a line and by flicking your card attempt to knock the cards down that had been placed up against the wall. The boy who knocked the last one down picked up all the cards. Of course you can imagine these cards used to get rather grubby.

A game we played usually after school we called it 'Fox and Hounds'. The idea was that two boys were chosen as foxes and they would set off, sometimes over the Mount, in fact anywhere in Henley. The other boys were the hounds and it was up to them to find and catch the two boys who were the foxes. If you played around your own home someone would surely find you a job and if the policeman saw you out after dark he would send you home. I remember one night another boy and myself were the foxes and set off. We climbed the tree alongside the porch of St. John's Church and lay down on the porch roof. We had only been there a short while when a policeman came along and stood opposite looking down Beaudesert Lane. He was there for a good hour and we dare not move in case he spotted us. When he did finally go we got down but by this time the other boys had gone home.

Once a week my brothers and I would take it in turn to fetch my father's tobacco, he smoked twist 4½d an ounce. The tobacconist judged this ounce almost perfectly, cutting the amount from a stick of 'Twist'. Sometimes there would be a very small amount of tobacco left after the ounce had been cut off and the tobacconist would put this in at no extra charge. During the conker season we would bore a small hole into the conker and whenever there was that little bit of extra twist over we would rub it and press it into the hole. We would then bore another hole to connect with the first hole and into this second hole we would poke a short length of Michaelmas Daisy stem. We obtained matches and lit the tobacco and puffed away like a pipe.

We had no holidays but the school would take us out for odd days and one of the places they took us to was Ladbrook Park. We would go by train from Wootton to Wood End. There was a tower at the house and it was quite a thrill to be taken to the top and see the surrounding countryside. The house belonged to a Mr. Oscar Bowen. The day was taken up with sports and games.

To earn some money to help my father one of the jobs I did was to clean cutlery for a lady who kept a cafe on the corner of Station Road and the High Street. There were about a hundred knives, forks and spoons on which I used emery powder. For this I was paid a 1d. In the season I have picked primroses from Owls Wood, this was close to the junction of New Road and Mayswood Road. I did them up in small bunches and sold them to visitors who arrived by coach from Birmingham, most of whom were going on to Stratford — they usually stopped in Henley for some refreshments. Many's the time I have blacked my face and run alongside these coaches asking for a copper. I never kept any of this money, it all went to my father.

In the end my father had to go to the Board of Guardians for help and it was decided that my brother Frank and myself and two of my sisters should go into St. Edwards Home at Coleshill. I would be about ten years of age at this time and I remained in the home until I was fourteen.

Things were hard at the home, even at ten I was placed in charge of a small boy who would be about five. Each morning at six o'clock a Nun would enter the dormitory and clap her hands, that was the signal to get up and no one dared lie in. On getting up I would dress and wash, then go downstairs to see that my young charge was up and help to dress and wash him, then help him make his bed and then I would run back upstairs to make my own bed and do one of the many jobs we boys had to do to ensure that the dormitory was clean and tidy before we went to breakfast. For breakfast we had bread and margarine and cocoa. After breakfast we marched to school, no talking. St. Pauls was a very good school. We returned to the home for dinner which consisted of meat and vegetables all stewed up in the same pot which made up into a thick soup. For tea we had the same as for breakfast. We had one egg a year and that was served on Easter Sunday. On Christmas Day there were no toys. After dinner a banana was shared between three boys and if you were lucky you might get an apple.

I only left the home once during the four years I was there. This was with a number of other boys we were sent to Besford Court in Worcestershire. I believe the place was used as an office from which letters were sent out appealing for money. We boys would fold these letters and put them into envelopes and do any other little jobs we could to help the staff. One of them was very helpful to me and when I came to leave he gave me some money which I spent by putting the pennies into a chocolate machine on the station whilst waiting for the train to take us back to Coleshill. I got into trouble for this because it would seem that I should have handed the money over to the people at the home.

When it was time to go to bed at the home we would undress in the day room which was downstairs, except for just our trousers. We were then marched along the stone corridors and up concrete steps, we had nothing on our feet, up to our dormitory. We would stand by our beds until ordered to get into bed. It could be very cold during the winter.

We were expected to do our own mending. If for example you got a hole in your jersey you would be given an old jersey from which you would pick a strand of wool then you had to darn the hole as best as you could. Some boys were very good.

When I was fourteen the Board of Guardians obtained a job for me as assistant gardner at Clopton House, Stratford-on-Avon. I went into lodgings there. We worked six days a week. On Sundays I would go to Church then for a walk. I had little money to do anything else. The people I lodged with were very good to me. I cannot be sure how long I stayed at Clopton House, but I returned to Henley and lodged with one of my brothers.

I managed to get a job with Mr. Hazelwood who lived at "The Woodlands" Mayswood Road. I tended the gardens. Mr. Hazelwood was very good to young men because there was little for us to do after we had finished work. He would allow a certain number of us youngsters to come to his home once a week to play billiards or snooker and he would supply sandwiches and cocoa. I believe the boys had to be recommended by the Minister of the Baptist Church. I left Mr. Hazelwood after a while because in addition to looking after the garden he wanted me to care for his cattle. I liked animals but could never work with cows. I was fortunate enough to hear of a vacancy for a gardener at Glendossal which was a home for private mental patients and this is where the present Riverside School is situated. The wage was 25/- per week.

I then heard of a job going at Austey Manor offering accommodation which suited me as I had recently become married, this was in 1927. I secured the job which paid 40/- a week which was very good seeing that a cottage went with the job. Of course I was working almost seven days a week. The people I worked for were Mr. & Mrs. Williams. No so long after I had started I was approached by Mr. Williams who said that his wife's maid had left and Mrs. Williams wanted my wife to help at the home. This was something I had made clear to Mr. Williams when I accepted the job, that I was not prepared for my wife to work outside of our home. I

Henley Rat Club.
Some of the members with their dogs. The number 12,000 represented by dead rats
probably represents a milestone in the clubs history.
From left to right: Sid (pop) Taylor, Nip Bomber ? W. Bonehill, Les Jackson,
Harry Hughes, J. Beard, Bill Castle, J. Malins, Arthur Russell, Tommy O'Donnell
(Kneeling) W. Beard.

reminded Mr. Williams of this and he agreed that I had but his wife was
insisting that she was not prepared to engage another maid. The outcome
was that I was not prepared to give way on this point so we left. We moved
back into Henley, this would be about 1929 to a small cottage next to the
'Elms' in the High Street. We had one room downstairs and the smallest of
kitchens you could hardly get two people in. We had running water, lighting
was by oil. Our toilet was at the top of the garden, which was a very long
one. After a bonfire the ashes would be riddled and kept in a bucket with a
small shovel close to the toilet, after use you would spread some of the ash
over the humus. This was eventually spread over the garden.

About this time I joined the Warwickshire County Council. I worked for
them for forty years and was happy in my work. I was foreman for 22 years
of my service. I was mainly employed on road works. In the early days we
had to make our own way to work, mainly by push bike to such places as
Berkswell, Barford and Solihull. We had to report by 6.30 a.m. and worked
until five o'clock Monday to Friday. Saturdays we finished at four o'clock.
We were paid 6/- a day. I remember we used to get rises of 4d a day.

Holidays were one week each year. We got bank holidays but not Good Friday. If you wanted this day off you had to make it up by working extra hours on Saturdays.

In my early days you would come across what we called 'Stone Pickers'. Where fields had been ploughed you would find these men picking stones from the fields and putting them on the sides of the roads in rucks (heaps). These stone pickers would sit by the side of the road and with a long handled hammer break the larger stones into small pieces. We would then use these stones to fill in holes in the road with the help of turf and soil from the sides of the road, breaking the soil down fine to act as packing for the stones.

This was before we began to use tar. When tarring came in we were supplied with overalls and clogs, but I could never get on with these clogs so I used to keep an old pair of boots for this work. I don't remember the reason but chemicals were put into the tar and we found to begin with the steam from the tar affected our faces and brought the skin off just as if you had been sun burned. After a while our skins seem to get used to the steam from the tar. Tarring was done by spray and we used spreaders to even it out over the road. We tackled all sorts of jobs connected with roads and drains. When I was foreman I had to put in a daily report showing what we had done.

Just before I was due to retire the Divisional Surveyor came to see me to enquire whether I would be prepared to stay on. I worked it out that financially I would be little better off if I stayed working so I said I would retire. The Surveyor said he fully understood my reasoning and thanked me for all I had done but there was no other recognition from the Council. I am not complaining because as I have said I was always happy in my work and took a pride in my job.

Looking back over my life I have no regrets and would not have been born at any other time. My early years were hard but somehow we were always happy.

Sometime before the second World War a Rat Club was formed in Henley. Master of the Club was Pop Taylor. There were about a dozen of us, some had dogs, others had ferrets. We had a fixture secretary and his job would be to contact local farmers and arrange for us to pay a visit, usually on a Sunday morning. We would do all we could to get rid of as many rats as posible. The biggest catch was 435 in 2¾ hours at a farm near Barford. We used to wear yellow or gold coloured berries with H.R.C. printed on the front.

Ted O'Donnell died February 23rd, 1981.

Ted O'Donnell's Son Bernard is a former High Bailiff, and is at present Town Crier.

Lilian Beatrice Parkes

I was born 22nd March, 1915, in the same bedroom as my mother, over my grandfather's shop, which was situated where the present Henley Ice-Cream shop stands on the corner of the High Street and what is now School Road but which did not exist when I was born. Our garden ran back up to what is now Brook End Drive. At the back of the house were stables. My grandfather's shop sold toys and fancy goods. His name was E. Gould and he in fact was a carrier. I have a copy of the Arden News and Advertiser dated February 1891 price one half-penny, in which he has taken space and shows that he was a general carrier and coal dealer. It would seem also from this advert that he was the fore runner of the bus service because he states in his advert that he leaves Henley daily at 8 a.m. for Birmingham returning from the "Spread Eagle" Spiceal Street, Bull Ring at 4 p.m. My father was born at Four Oaks Farm, Buckley Green. I am not certain that this farm exists today. I had two brothers. I think my very first memory was falling on a bucket of coal which was outside the back door and cutting my head. My father wrapped me in a shawl and took me to the chemist, Mr Perkins, who put plasters on the cut. My first encounter with school was living so close I one day decided to follow the children into school — this was before I was of school age. One of the teachers happened to notice me playing with bricks and informed my mother who had become quite concerned because she was unable to find me. I was between four and five when I first went to school. Two teachers I remember were Miss Edna Mayland and Miss Simmonite, cannot be sure how her name was spelt but I can remember she went somewhere abroad as a Baptist Missionary. The headmaster was Mr. P. R. Walker. A lesson my Mother taught me from a very early age was always to take care of money and to save whenever possible. She would always try and give me a six pence each week to buy a savings stamp from my teacher. Somehow I have never forgotten the lesson. When I was 13 years of age I went to King's High School for Girls (Warwick) travelling each day by train. I remained at this school for four years. Latin and French were my best subjects, history and geography my worst. I cannot remember the exact year but possibly it was the late 20s or early 30s that my parents transferred their business to 197 High Street almost opposite our old business. The old property was sold to Mr. & Mrs. Hewins who carried on a dairy business.

My father somehow did a variety of part time jobs mainly clerical I seem to remember. He was a very keen organist and played for the Baptist Church in Henley to begin with. He was a pupil for some time of the Birmingham City Organist Mr. C. J. Perkins. I am told that around about 1907 he was asked to deputise for the organist at Tanworth Parish Church who was indisposed. This person apparently never recovered and my father remained as organist for 30 years. I understand that during the

THE ARDEN NEWS AND ADVERTISER.

| No. 6. | FEBRUARY, 1891. | PRICE ONE HALF-PENNY. |

GODRICH'S
GENERAL SUPPLY STORE,

Opposite the Church, HENLEY-IN-ARDEN, and at HOCKLEY HEATH,

THE CHEAPEST AND BEST STORE FOR

GROCERY, PROVISIONS, TINWARE, IRONWARE,

And FRUITS of every description.

Sole Agent for the Celebrated "MAZAWATTEE" CEYLON TEA.   A sample can be had free on application.

BON-BONS IN GREAT VARIETY.   PIPES, TOBACCO AND CIGARS.   HOME-CURED HAMS & BACON.

GUARANTEED Royal Daylight Petroleum 10d. per Gallon.   Special Quotations by the Barrel.
Don't buy commoner Oils which are sold for Best.

GOODS DELIVERED TO ANY PART BY OUR OWN CART.

WILLIAM SHAKESPEARE,
AVON House, HENLEY-IN-ARDEN,

The Largest Stock of

Flannels, Calicoes, Sheetings,
Quilts, Blankets, &c.,

in the Town.

1000 PAIRS BOOTS

To Select from.   Our Customers know the Quality.

MEN'S LEATHER LEGGINS.

New Stock of Men's & Boys' OVERCOATS.

Ladies' and Children's Ulsters from 1/6.

MEN'S SUITS from 14/6

Try our Measured Suits at 25s.

————o————

FLANNELETTS from 1¾d.

COCOA-MATTING.   CARPETS

ESTABLISHED 39 YEARS.

E. GOULD,

General Carrier & Coal Dealer,

HENLEY-IN-ARDEN,

Leaves Henley daily, at 8 a.m., for Birmingham,
returning from the "Spread Eagle," Spiceal Street,
Bull Ring, at 4 p.m.

ORDERS & COMMISSIONS PROMPTLY EXECUTED.

Please Address "PER GOULD."

FURNITURE CAREFULLY REMOVED

Truck Loads of Coal to any Station.

PRICES ON APPLICATION.

PIANOS and other INSTRUMENTS,
STRINGS, FITTINGS & REPAIRS,
At a fraction above Cost Price for Cash.

PIANOS, ORGANS, &c., for HIRE or DEFERRED PAYMENTS

F. G. FAIRFIELD'S
MUSIC WAREHOUSE,

High Street, SOLIHULL,

For First-Class TUNING & REPAIRS,

RECOMMENDED BY

Mr. ·, R GAUL, Mus. Bac., Mr. T. ANDERTON, Mus. Bac.
Mr. COURTENAY WOODS, R.A.M.,

And Employed by the Principal Residents in North and
Central Warwickshire.

SEND FOR PRICE LISTS AND TESTIMONIALS.

whole of this time he only missed one service. Unfortunately my father died as the result of a motor cycle accident on January 20th, 1937. He was on his way to Tanworth to play the organ and it is believed that he skidded on the icy road, no one witnessed the accident he was found lying in the road.

My mother died during October 1948.

Beatrice Parkes died in January, 1990.

Mary Pugh

I was born in a cottage in the main street of Ullenhall almost opposite Crowley's Farm on May 20th, 1901 and christened Mary. I have no idea why I was given only one Christian name whereas my three brothers each had two. I had two sisters in addition to my three brothers.

My grandparents came to Ullenhall in 1897 from Rous Lench, that was where my two eldest brothers were born. My Grandfather had been bailiff to the Bomfords who farmed and had business interests near Bidford.

My Grandfather, when he came to Ullenhall, took over Heath Farm as a tenant of Cannon Newton, brother of Squire Newton of Barells Hall. My father brought his family to Ullenhall soon after. The village as I first remember it was just cottages on our side of the Street down to Brook Cottage, a few houses along Watery Lane, there were no houses from Crowley's Farm until you came to the School. Then along the Henley Road on the left hand side there was only Park Barn which was occupied by Mr. Pottle, who was head gardener at Barrells Hall. On the other side of the road there were just open fields between Church Hill and the lodge at Barrells.

We had about six street lamps, lit by oil of course; these were attended to by Ralph Franklin.

Squire Newton was responsible for building our Church, St. Mary's in 1875. He also had our school built.

One of my earliest memories was the fear I had of going to school for the first time yet I already had two brothers at the school. However I soon forgot my fear. There were six classes and I would think about eighty children who apart from Ullenhall would come from the surrounding districts, some came quite a way and they had to walk whatever the weather. Our ages were from about five up to fourteen.

Miss Hannah Crooks was our headmistress and Miss Annie Albrighton one of the teachers, who in addition to taking the normal subjects, also took singing and sewing. Miss Crooks was a wonderful person, very strict, she would cane boys who were taller than she was. I was disciplined on occasions mostly for talking when I should have been listening. Punishment

Main Street, Ullenhall. Winged Spur Inn on right just beyond gathering of children. The lady in the fore-ground is standing on the site which was later to become Central Stores.

Barrells Hall, 1914 (Ullenhall).

usually took the form of standing out in front of the class, but not facing them, with hands on head for possibly five or ten minutes.

I think it must have been during the summer months, but once a week the girls would go to Henley School for cookery lessons for the whole day, and the boys would also go to Henley for carpentry but they would only go for half a day. Our walk to Henley would take us over 13 fields, some were only small.

My mother would always give us a penny each Monday morning to take to school which went into a savings scheme but I cannot remember what happened to the money when I came to leave school.

I cannot remember our parents giving us any pocket money, the money we spent on sweets was usually the result of running an errand for someone.

Mr. & Mrs. Newton were very kind people. At Christmas we children were invited to the Hall and in the servants hall there would be a wonderful Christmas tree. We would have a very nice tea and before we went home each boy would be given a jersey and the girls a length of material sufficient to make a dress. The last year that I was at school we girls were given a cloak, mine was red.

Mrs. Newton started a Scout group and the Squires two sisters were responsible for having the Coffee House built, which is situated at the corner of Church Hill and the Main Street. The property today still bears the name 'Coffee House'. It was a centre for all sorts of activities, especially for young people, otherwise there was nowhere for them to go. All sorts of games could be played — billiards, draughts and dominoes. They also formed a 'Band of Hope Society'. For the older people there were whist drives, 3 prizes, entrance 6d. Dances were also 6d. Coffee and soft drinks were served, but no alcohol. The Womens Institute was started in the Coffee House in 1927.

Our Baker was a Mr. Chattaway. His shop was where Mr. Ives grocery and news-agent shop was, unfortunately he has closed down. Mr. Chattaways assistant was a Mr. Allcott who delivered bread and cakes by horse and van, visiting many of the outlying villages and hamlets. After a time Mr. Allcott decided to go into business on his own account as a baker. He opened his premises next to the garage, opposite Church Hill, the property is still named 'the old bakery'. Mr. Allcott proved to be very successful and took many awards in the Midlands and at national exhibitions for his bread and pies.

Tommy Stanton was our postman. He would set out from Henley making deliveries on the south side of Henley and then making his way over to Mayswood then on to Oldberrow, Ullenhall, Dansey Green then back to Henley, what a walk. He would always bring three copies of the Birmingham Post newspaper with him, one for my father, but I am not sure who the other two were for. Mr. William Washington Richards was our post-master, he also sold grocery and sweets. My elder brothers have often

St. Mary The Virgin Church (C of E), Ullenhall.

earned themselves 4d for delivering a telegram to one of the outlying farms or houses.

A Mr. Course had the Central Stores built which in addition to selling grocery also had a wine and spirits licence. I don't think Mrs. Course was very happy with the accommodation because she was very fond of gardening and I don't think there is any garden with this property.

Our vicar was the Rev. W. F. Pelton who was in charge of the parish from 1901 until 1932, his young son was born in the same year as I was. The vicar always called me Molly. I don't know why because no one else did. There was an occasion when Mr. Pelton called on my parents and brought with him something which turned out to be shirt material. He turned to me and said 'Molly I want you to make me three shirts'. Whilst I was reasonably good at sewing and making frocks I had never made a shirt 'I said I can't make shirts' but all he would say was 'You will manage'. From time to time an elderly friend of my parents would come and stay with us for a few days. On her last visit, by coincidence she had left behind a pattern for shirts. Somehow I was able to follow this pattern and eventually finished one shirt. When I showed it to Mr. Pelton he said 'fit for the Lord Mayor' so I got away with that problem.

My father and two eldest brothers all sang in the church choir. In our church the pews were allocated to local farmers and their families and also the gentry. You can still see the marks of the cards where they were placed on the narrow shelf where you normally place you hymn and prayer book.

I left school when I was fourteen and for the first year or so I was kept fairly busy assisting my mother and making my own clothes and doing similar work for other people.

Just beyond the village on the road leading to the Alcester-Birmingham Road on the left hand side is a massive tree called 'Crowleys Oak'. No one seems to know where the name 'Crowley' came from or how old this Oak tree is but it is reckoned to be several hundred years old. As children it was a favourite haunt of ours, we would always be attempting to climb this tree.

The house which now stands behind this rather famous tree takes its name from the tree and is called 'Crowleys Oak'. A Mrs. Grant-Ferris had this house built for her son Robert who was to become a member of Parliament and subsequently 'Speaker of the House of Commons'. He later became Lord Harvington, taking his title from Harvington Hall which is a property belonging to the Roman Church. Lord Harvington's son Piers is a priest in the R.C. Church. We still correspond with each other at Christmas time. Mrs. Grant-Ferris was a great benefactor of Harvington Hall, which is near Kidderminster. Mr. Sumner of Typhoo Tea Company once lived at Crowley's Oak.

We had two tradesmen who would call at fairly frequent intervals. Mr. Morris, for grocery items and Mr. Heaphy with Haberdashery. They came from Redditch on their bicycles, take any orders which would be delivered later by horse and van.

I think I would be about 17 or 18 when I first met Mr. Chadwick the artist, more famous now than he was then. You could often see him cycling around the village on his way to paint some scene or perhaps a property. On one occasion I met him painting and said that I liked what he was painting. He said 'you must visit my studio when you come to Henley,' it was above the drapers 'Herrings' close to the White Swan. When I did eventually visit his studio I picked out a paintaing which I said I liked and he said, 'that for me it would be £5' I said 'I cannot possibly afford that' so I came away without any picture. Some time later I received a letter from Mr. Chadwick telling me that if I was still interested in the picture that I had pointed out then I could have it for £2.10.0d which I did buy and which you can see hanging in my lounge.

I was housekeeper to Mr. & Mrs. Power for 16/17 years. Soon after the first World War my father started a cricket team in Ullenhall, they played in a meadow just behind the present village hall. I remember that Alf. Woodward and Harry Lowe from Henley played in this team, occasionally Robert Grant-Ferris would play. No one had a car, we used to cycle to play games at the surrounding villages, the men would carry their bats, pads and stumps on their bicycles. I used to help make the tea, we used two spirit stoves given to us by our vicar Rev Pelton.

My father had originally bought Yew Tree Farm in Ullenhall but about

1930 he bought Oldberrow Hill Farm because it was larger than Yew Trees. We lived there for about 20 years but following my fathers death we moved back to Ullenhall.

In 1937 we had a severe winter with so much snow that in places it was level with the tops of the hedges. It was quite impossible to get through to the Alcester Road.

During the second World War the W.I. made 800 lbs of Jam and we only had oil stoves to cook with. We also knitted garments for the forces. In 1942 Mrs. Helena Roosevelt visited Ullenhall to see how the Land Girls were coping. She was apparently very interested in farming. She was staying at Broadway during her visit.

Mary died on 24th December, 1992.

Annie May Savage (Nee Elvins)

I was an only child born at Rowley Regis, Staffordshire, November 15th, 1901. My mother and Father moved to Henley about 1906, my father to become Bailiff at Preston Bagot Farm. We lived to begin with at 201 High Street later moving to 74 High Street which was a small sweet shop. We also sold a little grocery and tobacco.

My earliest memory is going to school with Alice Hemming, we remained firm friends until she died. My first teacher was a Mrs. Argyle who I remember with affection as always kind and a very good teacher. Alice's father had a shop at No. 160 High Street where he sold good quality furniture and also crockery. They also made coffins. Going to school we would skip or bowl our wooden hoops whichever happened to be in fashion. I cannot think what we did with our hoops once we got to school but our ropes we would fold up and hang on our coat pegs in the cloakroom. Hop-scotch was a favourite pastime, chalking the numbers on the surface of the playground. We had open fires at school and if you should happen to have a cold you were allowed to sit close to the fire. We had book prizes at the end of each term for the best pupils in various subjects. I can remember winning prizes for geography, painting and sewing. Flos. Kirby would take us for sewing and needlework. Mr. Robinson was our head-master, who was very strict. He would walk round the class with one hand behind his back holding a cane which would be hidden up the back of his jacket. I cannot remember how it was that Mr. & Mrs. Robinson, who lived in Stratford, once invited a number of us children to tea. Mr. Robinson was quite a different person at home to the one we knew at school. Whilst we had no holidays during my time at school I was more fortunate than a good many children. We had relatives in the

Rowley Regis area who we visited which was quite an outing. My mother would also take me occasionally to Birmingham to shop. I can remember going to Barretts, a store my mother favoured for shoes, where she would buy me brown lace up boots. The laces would pass through holes until you came up to three little metal tags either side, these tags were just little right angles pieces of metal which you would put the lace round. I don't really know why the boots had these tags because holes would have served just the same purpose. After a while these metal tags frayed the laces which in turn would break just as you were getting ready to go to school. A very nice feature of these trips to Birmingham was a visit to the Hen & Chickens which was a very pleasant little restaurant where my mother would order tea with muffins, scones and jam. In the summer there was cream. My mother would also ask for a dish of plain cakes. I always wondered why we could not have cream cakes to which my mother replied that plain cakes were better for you.

Like most people my parents kept a pig. After it was killed the sides would be laid in a sort of sink which I think was called a tram, made up of blue bricks. Salt and salt petre would be well rubbed in. These sides of pork and bacon would be hung up in the kitchen with a piece of heavy paper between them and the wallpaper to prevent any grease going on to the wallpaper. Neighbours would purchase some of the joints and my mother would make some pork pies which Mr. Welch the baker would put in his ovens. To replace the killed pig my father would approach anyone he knew whose sow had just given birth to a litter to see whether he could purchase what was called the 'dillings' the weakest of the litter, which with a little luck could be bought for 5/-.

As a young girl I enjoyed helping my mother with the cooking, there were little things I could do. I also assisted with housework, it was never a chore, I enjoyed it and still do. In those days I would, among other jobs, clean the knives, forks and spoons, this was in the days before stainless steel. If you did not look after your cutlery it would soon discolour. During my school days I took piano lessons from Miss Beck which went on for about two years. I was getting on reasonably well but I cannot now remember why these lessons should have stopped. My mother was not keen on my playing in the street after tea so I would generally visit friends and play in their house or garden. We played with our dolls and we enjoyed making clothes for them. Christmas was always a time we looked forward to. We made all our own decorations, paper chains from coloured strips of paper, using flour and water as paste. We would also purchase squares of coloured paper which we used to pull from the centre which made it into a cone, then we would sow these cones together from the centre which came into a ball shape. We would decorate a piece of ivy and hang it from the ceiling, which would act as our Christmas tree. Most of these coloured papers we purchased from a Miss Chetters who kept a little shop at 121 High Street, who sold mostly stationery but at Christmas time she would have all seasonal gifts, not very expensive, set out on tables and shelves in what was their living room. It was most exciting for us children to walk round and gaze at all the things which were for sale. The butchers' shop at this time would also display their poultry outside.

There were Sunday School outings which were always something to look forward to. We would go to Haven Pastures which at that time was lived in by a Mr. Walter Richmond. There were organised games and races. In those days of limited travel the going and coming back was all part of the treat. I think we would go by Johnson's horse and cart.

When I reached 14 years of age a bachelor uncle of mine who lived in London paid for me to spend a weeks holiday with an aunt and her son at Colwyn Bay. I can still remember the name of the guest house where we stayed 'Leeds House'. I remember the donkey rides and the donkey cart rides we enjoyed. There was one little incident which remains as a memory of that holiday and that was that my cousin and I seemed to spot what appeared to be a gold bracelet lying on the sands. We both made a grab for it at the same time and neither of us would let go until my aunt parted us and took the bracelet. Later she gave it to me but I am sure it was only rolled gold. I stayed at school until I was nearly sixteen years of age, so did Alice Hemming the first girl I remember going to school with. My first job was with Rushton's the Chemists who were on the parade at Hall Green in Birmingham, close to the station. I travelled by train daily from Henley catching the 7.55 a.m. which got me to Hall Green Station a few minutes after the shop had opened at 8.30 a.m. The shop remained open until 8 p.m. but I was allowed to leave a few minutes before this in order to catch the train back to Henley which I reached at about 8.45 p.m. My commencing wages were 7/6d per week, although after a months service Mr. Rushton raised my salary to 10/- per week. When I left at 18 years, due to my mothers death I was earning 15/- per week. Mrs Rushton always made me a cup of cocoa to have with my sandwiches at lunch time. I was not keen on cocoa but did not have the courage to tell her.

I enjoyed the work I did for Mr. Rushton. In addition to serving in the shop the other assistants and I were employed in weighing up such things as epson salts, globa salts, bi-carbonate, borax, bismuth mixture into 1 oz and 2 oz packs.

Pills were produced by a small machine, the ingredients being made up into a soluble mixture, rolled by hand and then fed into the machine. You never knew really whether the pills were going to be identical in appearance. Tincture of Quinnine came in glass containers referred to as Winchesters. In 1918 at the height of the flu epidemic we hardly did anything else but make up bottles of this mixture. Rushtons had a very good cough mixture containing linseed and lobelia which customers spoke very well of. We hardly sold any cosmetics in those days.

After leaving Rushtons I stayed at home and kept house for my father. After a year or two I went out to work again, this time I joined a Mrs. Jones

The same bridge as referred to by Mrs. Savage but not the same boys.

who had a confectionary and cooked meats shop in Sparkhill, Birmingham. Most of my leisure time was spent going walks, naturally we spoke to boys of our own age who would often congregate at the little bridge just beyond the Golden Cross. There was the odd excursion from Henley Station to places like Weston-Super-Mare, 5/-d return.

About 1924 I joined Mr. J. Welch who ran the bakery business, the shop is still the home-made bakery only under different management. I was 17 years with Mr. Welch. We worked hard but we were all very happy.

I was married in 1931 and Mr. Welch paid for and arranged the wedding reception which was held in the large tea room at the rear of the shop. I was married at St. Nicholas Church by Mr. Easterbrook, the Rector. Miss Geary was the organist. The marriage fee was 15/6d.

Whilst at Welch's as I have said we were busy for most of the time. We commenced work at 8 a.m. although I did not start until 9 a.m. We would work through until 7 p.m. and on Saturdays it was 9 p.m. Our work consisted mainly for the early part of the week cleaning all the shelves and looking after a small tea room we had which was to the left of the main shop, and then you were serving for most of the rest of the time. We had a customer who kept a small cafe at Hockley Heath and she ordered cakes from us which we would put up in a box and the Midland Red Bus would stop and pick up the box and deliver it to the cafe in Hockley Heath. For this service we would purchase a stamp from Katie Stevens Stationery shop, who were Midland Red Agents. Another customer for our cakes was a Mrs. Rollins of Tanworth who I believe had a small shop and usually had a tray of our cakes delivered late on Friday for sale on Saturday. My first home after becoming married was at 138 High Street which a Mrs. Warwick rented to us for 12/6d per week plus 1/6d annual rent for the bay window. I believe this was referred to as a Tythe payment. When we decorated, my husband took as many as eight papers from some of the walls. We were here for about six years before Mrs. Warwick returned to Henley and required her cottage for herself. In 1936 we moved to Lapworth where my husband had accepted a job at Lapworth Court. As a result I only continued at Welch's on a part-time basis.

Soon after the outbreak of the second World War we were asked to take in two little evacuees from Birmingham. They stayed with us for only a few months before returning to their homes. We were then asked to take two girls from the East End of London. Although this episode was over fifty years ago we still maintain contact with those little girls who now have homes of their own. I remember that some Saturdays we would take them to the cinema in Knowle which was four miles away and we would walk there and back.

In 1959 we moved back to Henley buying ourselves a small bungalow in which we still live.

I have never been one for joining organisations, I have helped at many functions and was happy to do so. Somehow I have always been happy and contented in my own home, there has always seemed to be plenty to occupy me, despite the fact that my husband and I never had a family. Looking back on life it may not have been particularly eventful but I have been happy and in many ways fortunate and have no regrets at being born when I was.

Mr. Savage died in 1986.

Mary Ellen Townsend (nee Howard)

I was born on the 22nd Jun, 1902 at Clopton Lodge at the entrance to Clopton House, Stratford-upon-Avon which at that time was occupied by Sir Arthur Hodgson. My father worked as a gardener for Sir Arthur.

My mother was born in Stratford-upon-Avon and my father came from Snitterfield. My mother's first child was a boy. Sir Arthur asked my parents before the christening what name they had decided on and was told 'George Harold', his reply was that the boy should be named John after his father. Unfortunately my brother died at the age of six months. I was born next

The very young Mrs. Townsend outside Edstone Hall.

and my sister came four years later. When I was about two or three my father had an opportunity to better himself and we moved to the lodge at Edstone Hall near Bearley which at that time was occupied by a Mr. Pearson who was connected with the Coal and Coke Company, Wilson, Carter & Pearson of Birmingham. Mr. Pearson would go to Bearley Station by pony and trap and then by train to Birmingham. He always wore a flower in his button hole and I can see my mother opening the lodge gates when he left for his office.

We lived in the lodge which had cellars, one had a copper where my mother would do her washing, using a candle to provide the light. There was no gas or electricity in those days. Our toilet was in the woods. When my sister was born I would be about four years old and I can remember my mother giving me a note to take to a neighbour who lived quite some way along the main Stratford Road, a Mrs. Payne. Can you imagine a child of four being allowed to walk along the road today? Of course there was only horse traffic at that time. The road was not nearly so wide as it is today and the surface was rough stone. There were more trees than there are now. I can see the six-in-hand coach and horses going by on their way to Stratford. I never knew whether it was for my benefit but the man sitting on top at the rear of the coach would always give a blast on his long horn as they passed the lodge. My sister was christened at Wootton Wawen Church and whilst I remember little of the actual ceremony I can recall being carried on my Uncle's shoulder to the church. It was quite a step from Edstone Lodge to Wootton Church but all the family walked there and back.

The main road to Stratford-on-Avon with Wootton Mill on the left. A scene that would have been similar to the one Mary Townsend describes on the journey to her sisters Christening at Wootton Wawen Church.

We had relatives in Stratford and when they came to visit us my mother would take us to Bearley Station to meet them. My sister would be in a pram and I would trot alongside. When it was time for our relatives to return home my father, being the gardener at Edstone, would always give these relatives a bunch of flowers to take home with them. I do not know why but I could not bear to see those flowers being given away and I used to create such a scene. In the end I think my parents would still hand the flowers over but not in front of me, which I presume solved that problem. I have always throughout my life been passionately fond of flowers and their arrangement.

When the mop visited Stratford we would visit our relatives this was always an occasion for the family to come together. One of my aunts worked at the Shakespeare Hotel. This aunt would send out for 2/6d worth of pork from the pig roast, we would then have baked potatoes, brussel sprouts and stuffing which was delicious.

Although I never realised the value at the time, one of the visitors who came to see Mr. Pearson gave me a half sovereign. I used to carry this around in a small purse which one day I left on top of the water butt which was situated by the lodge gates close by the road. When I next remembered to look for the purse it could not be found. Some days afterwards it was found in the hedge bordering the main road, unfortunately my half sovereign had gone. We could only think that perhaps a tramp had been passing and spotted my purse. There were plenty of tramps in those days passing along the road. There was the workhouse at Stratford situated at the rear of the present out-patients department of the Stratford hospital where tramps could get a nights' lodging. At Christmas time Mrs. Pearson would send mince pies to my mother and sweets for us children. I can also remember receiving an Eskimo Doll from Granny Lodder (late F. S. Lodder's mother). She would also bring us mince pies and knitted bed socks. She was also responsible for enrolling my mother and other women into the Mothers Union. Mr. Bramston, Vicar at Wootton Wawen would visit us periodically.

Each Christmas my mother would tell my sister and I the Christmas Story, we loved this. My father would also tell us stories, most of which we had heard before but we never tired of hearing them again. On Christmas Eve we would hang up our black knitted stockings. There was much excitement the following morning to find an apple, orange, sugar pig or mouse. New pennies, handkerchief with father christmas printed on them. If we were lucky we might get a small doll but we never looked for anything big. When I was about five, Mr. Pearson died and Mrs. Pearson moved to Leamington Spa. My father still continued to work for her. I went to Rugby Road School as soon as I was five. In Leamington I can remember that Gamages had a store where Rackhams is to-day. Francis's and Burgess and Colbourne were also established stores in the town.

After only a year or so Mrs. Pearson died and her son moved to Nunhold Grange near Hatton. We followed, living in the gardeners' cottage. My sister and I went to school at Hatton which was two or three miles from where we lived. My sister hated going to school and quite often I had to carry her for much of the way. We would take sandwiches for our lunch but we were not very big eaters and quite often we would bring them home again. We carried a spare pair of shoes with us in case it rained and we got our feet wet, we could then change them when we got to school. We were fortunate and had an umbrella but some children would have a piece of sacking put round their shoulders to keep the rain from penetrating their clothes. If the weather was too bad my mother would keep us at home. The school-board man would call to inquire why we had not attended school but he seemed to be satisfied with my mother's explanation concerning the weather.

Whilst my father was at Nunhold Grange he would often walk to St. Mary's Church in Warwick. This was quite a walk for my father but he could tell my mother within a few minutes as to what time he would be home. He would also walk across the fields to visit his mother who lived in Snitterfield. Sometimes my sister and I would go with him. I think it was about 1910 that my father gave up his job with Mr. Pearson, Jnr. There was some disagreement with the house-keeper who had engaged the services of another gardener who was to be over my father. His next job was with Mr. Chappell (Piano firm) who lived at Wellesbourne Hall. To get this job he had to walk from Nunhold Grange to Wellesbourne.

Whilst at Wellesbourne I can remember going in to Stratford by Carriers Cart. There were fowl in crates on top, dead rabbits hanging from the sides, paraffin cans in the middle and butter and eggs from the various farms for sale in Stratford. There were seats either side of the cart for the passengers.

We were not at Wellesbourne for very long when my father took a job at Chadshunt Hall, Nr. Kineton. One item we had was a cylinder type gramophone with brass horn. We would take this to a nearby farm where there were other children. The record we liked best was "The whistler and his dog". We would play this over and over again, dancing like mad round a table. Whilst at Chadshunt Hall we attended Gaydon School but I don't have any memories of our time there. Whilst we were there we did have an aunt who lived in Leicester come to see us and stayed for a week. We went into Stratford whilst she was visiting us and I can remember her buying some Oxford type shirt material out of which my mother made my father three shirts, all by hand, she did not have a machine. On the subject of making things my mother somehow came by a red tunic, I think it must have been from the Boer War. She cut this up and made a little bodice for both my sister and I which we were very proud of. My mother never wasted any material which could be used. Whenever we visited Stratford we would always visit "Smiths" (now Debenhams). Mr. Robert Smith would always come up and speak to his customers. I remember they would have boots and shoes attached to boards hanging down either side of the entrance. Another well known shop in Stratford was Loggins the Chemist, this was before there was any 'Boots'. If folk knew you were going into Stratford and they wanted something from the chemist they would say get me so and so from Loggins.

Mitchells the bakers in Wood Street (now under different management) but still a bakers' shop, sold in addition to bread and cakes, faggots, chicklings and scratchings.

Still in Stratford I can remember the footpath being opened which connects Guild Street with Henley Street, coming out by the side of the Library. We thought it was wonderful to walk along this new thoroughfare.

In 1912 or thereabouts we moved out of Warwickshire to Gloucestershire to the small village of Bromsberrow where my father began work for a Major Webb. I think my most vivid memory of this place was the profusion of daffodils that grew around this area. At Easter time we picked and filled a clothes basket with daffodils and my father made three crosses which were placed in the windows of the local Church. We also sent a box of daffodils to our auntie who was living at Gas Cottage in Henley. She used them to decorate the Font at St. Nicholas Church in Henley.

Mrs. Webb was very good to us children at Christmas, there were about forty children in the school. She would supply a large Christmas tree for our party and each boy would get a blue cloak and the girls a red cloak. The year I was there I was a little disappointed because I received a cardigan.

Before the Christmas party a number of us children decided to walk to Eastnor Castle and sing Carols. Although we knocked at the door we did not see anyone so we came away empty handed. We did sing some carols at the various farms we passed on our way home and received a few coppers which we spent on sweets. My father eventually found us sliding on the local pond which had become frozen over. He was not too pleased when he heard what we had been up to. Another memory of this area was seeing the farm workers setting off with their horses each morning. Each man seemed to have a small barrel with a leather carrying handle which I learned later contained cider which they hung on the haimes of the horses collar. You could get eggs from the local farms round about Easter — 16 for 1/-.

We came to Henley in May 1914 and lived at 191 High Street. My mother had become a little homesick for Warwickshire. My father went to work for the Miss Knights, there were three sisters and they lived at Brook End House.

I went to the local school in the High Street. I was very happy at this school. One subject I was good at was composition. I can remember an occasion when Nutty Beard was caned, he was often in trouble but was never upset at being punished, but on this one occasion he was really upset which was most unusual. He said he had not done whatever he had been caned for. In the end it turned out that he was innocent and the head-master, Mr. Robinson apologised which was also very unusual. Mr. Robinson then said to our class I want you to write a composition on the subject "Is punishment necessary?." I won this little competition.

One amusing occasion occurs to me, it concerns a Mr. Busby who kept a greengrocery shop at 199 High Street. He was standing at the entrance to his shop, he was a small man with a moustache and wore a blue apron. The children called him Goosgog behind his back. One day a group of boys were passing as Mr. Busby stood in the doorway, one called out 'how are you Goosegog'. Mr. Busby chased this boy all the way into school, where he was caned for his rude remarks.

My teacher was a Miss Kirby whose parents kept the ironmongers where Dillon now stands.

The paving in the High Street was of blue bricks. Between them and the road were cobble stones. As children we used to push our peg tops into the earth between the cobbles and then whip them to get them spinning. You could earn yourself a penny or two by weeding between the cobbles from some people who lived along the High Street. At Beaudesert Park a Mr. & Mrs Richardson ran a preparatory school for boys. They wore green and white ribbon round their boaters. Every other Sunday they would march to St. Nicholas Church to attend the morning service.

Mrs. Richardson was very good to our school at Christmas. She would arrange for Welch's the bakers to provide the school with a very large iced Christmas cake. A few days before the Christmas holiday it would be placed in the widow of Welch's. News of its appearance would spread like wild-fire through the school. After school we would all be off to go and peer at this cake in the window. A sign that Christmas was not far away. At the school party we would receive an orange and a bag of sweets. It was a lovely time. Arden House School would use St. Johns Church every other Sunday, this was before the two churches were united.

One of my earliest war memories (1914 – 1918) was seeing Mr. P. Hawkes (local butcher) and Major Tibbets with a company of men all mounted and looking very smart come out of the side entrance of their shop. I suppose they would be off to Budrook Barracks at Warwick. I don't know when this would be but we heard that one of the City Battalions would be staying in Henley and people were asked to accommodate the troops. Where people agreed the soldiers number was chalked on the front door. On some houses there were two or three numbers showing on the front door, but there was one house where about six numbers were shown, it was only a small cottage and we wondered where the soldiers would sleep. The troops equipment was parked in the meadow alongside the brook on the east side of the High Street. The troops held various exercises whilst they were here in the fields where Cherry Orchard Estate is now and also out towards Crocketts Farm. The morning the troops were due to leave, they were all lined up by the Market Cross and the High Bailiff Mr. Nelson wished them farewell and good luck. Another occasion when troops visited Henley our father took us up the Birmingham Road by the white rails to see the Horse Artillery ride in. These horses looked marvellous and the guns and carriages were so smart, I felt we must win the war. They only stopped one night.

One night a Zeppelin came over, I suppose it was on its way to Birmingham. My Uncle came round to our house and to wake us he tapped on our bedroom window, which was upstairs, with a line prop. He and my Aunt lived in the Gas Cottage and were afraid of the gas works being hit. It was unlikely that the Germans ever knew the works existed. However we all crowded into the pantry under the stairs, we felt safe although there was little protection if anything had fallen on us.

My mother used to take in washing from such places as Arden House School and Glendossal Mental Home, also the Yew Trees. From the school she would get 45 sheets and 45 grey flannel shirts each week. From

Glendossal she would have night dresses. Most of these items were boiled in the copper, transferred to the tub where my mother used a dolly and finally each item was mangled. The drying of clothes was not too much of a problem during the summer months but when it was wet and through the winter, I have known my mother sit up all night turning the clothes in front of the fire. I am sure that my mother had about fourteen flat irons. My aunt from Beaudesert would often help my mother with the washing. I remember my mother using Sunlight Soap, Robbins Starch and Ricketts Blue. She would also take in other washing, table clothes came from the Rev. Lane.

My sister and I on a Saturday morning would carry the clothes basket back to Glendossal for which my father would always give us a penny. We used to spend this on a ½d rock cake which we bought from Mr. Hodges the baker, next to the Red Lion. Then we would go across the road to a little sweet shop run by Mrs. Stevens which was almost opposite the Red Lion. My favourite sweet was what we called Jap Nougat, small coloured squares with nutty flavour. There were boiled sweets in the shape of fishes, different colours, pear drops, raspberry drops and there was also imitation meat chops, peas and potatoes. My mother was not too keen on us having these, she was not happy about the colouring which was used. Toffee came in trays which Mrs. Stevens would break using a small hammer.

Mr. Samuel Agar was in charge of Glendossal and he would pay my mother and all other trades people on the first Monday of each month. He would call your name and in you went, signed the receipt and that was that.

My father had an allotment along the Ullenhall Road just beyond the railway bridge. He was required by the Miss Knights during the day to exercise their dog. He was not very keen on doing this so he would take the dog along to the allotment and tie him to a long lead then he would set about doing a little work on his allotment. Glendossal also had allotments near to my fathers. Mr. Agar used to take some of the lady patients along to do some work as part of their treatment. He would take lemonade for the patients and they seemed to enjoy the outing. My father said that all the doors at Brook End House, even the coal house were of solid oak. Another mental home was situated on the corner of Doctors Row and the High Street. I think it was called Doctors Row because of this home. People if they could afford it would pay into a sick club. This meant they could call the doctor or have the nurse if a baby was expected, otherwise they usually made do with the neighbour to deliver a baby. If it became really necessary to have the doctor and you were not in a sick club it usually meant calling on the more well to do people and asking if you could beg a sick ticket as you wanted to call the doctor but did not have the money to pay for his service. Very few if any refused such a request.

An event which caused great excitement was when Fossetts Circus returned from their summer tour to take up winter quarters in Beaudesert Lane just over the brook on the right hand side where there was a small meadow. Sometimes the ponies and horses would be allowed to graze in the

HRE.18F   VIEW FROM ST.JOHN'S CHURCH TOWER, HENLEY-IN-ARDEN

Beaudesert Lane with the meadow on the right providing winter quarters for Fossetts Circus and the meadow on the left grazed by the ponies and horses as remembered by Mary Townsend.

Rectory meadow which was opposite. There was also much activity in the Spring before the Circus set out for another tour. Carts and other items connected with the Circus were re-painted in very attractive colours.

The Police Station was manned day and night. There was a very smart Sergeant who carried a silver topped cane. Any suspicious character who appeared in Henley was followed until they left the town. Fireman were alerted of any fire by the Town Crier who would ride his bike up the street, clanging his bell and making suitable announcements. The fire engine was drawn by two horses who first had to be caught from their field, harnessed and then off they would race to the scene of the fire. Mr. Rund of the Little House, next to the Red Lion, usually supplied the horses. Early morning in Henley was a busy time with milkmen taking their milk by pony and float to the station to catch the early train round about 6.30 a.m.

Our streets, although there was only the High Street and Beaudesert Lane, were lit by gas supplied from the local gas works at the end of Beaudesert Lane. Blackford Pastures did not exist in my school days, neither did Cherry Orchard. Where the present Catholic School now stands (Arden Road) grew some lovely cowslips and purple orchids. I would pick armfuls and take them to people who were unwell.

When I reached the age of 14 years I obtained a job with Mr. & Mrs. Perkins who had the Chemist shop which was exactly where it is today. The shop then was not as large as it is today, there were two or three steps up

The Bicycle shop on the corner of Bear Lane was part of the Newcombe establishment. Adverts alongside the first floor windows are in support of Raleigh and B.S.A bikes. The soldiers are convalescing and come from the Public Hall which had been turned into a hospital during the first World War.

into the shop. One of my first jobs was to clean those steps. I commenced work at 7 a.m. After the steps I would light fires and scrub floors. I would work until three o'clock, return home and then come back again at four thirty p.m. to get the tea and work on until six o'clock, when the shop closed. The left hand side of the present shop was living accommodation. Mrs. Perkins would hold scripture lessons on a Tuesday evening in her living room. It was surprising the number of young people who attended these meetings. Mrs. Perkins would take certain passages form the Bible and explain the meaning. Even today when I am in Church I hear some of those same passages, I am straight away carried back in time to those meetings. Mrs. Perkins was a marvellous person. One thing that stands out in my memory about working for the Perkins, was that it was the time of the Great War. Most evenings after work I was required to take a box of medicine to the Public Hall (now Memorial Hall) which was being used as a convalescent home for wounded soldiers. As a young girl some of the soldiers would make the odd comment, usually complimentary. Then there used to be a seat outside the Bear Public House, corner of Bear Lane and High Street where soldiers would sit. It was nice at that age to be noticed.

After a year or so I secured a job with a Mrs. Ryland who lived at Preston Bagot House. I remember hiring a bike from a shop where the Othello restaurant now is, to go and see Mrs. Ryland. I secured the job, my starting wages being 13/4d per month. I was earning £2.6.8d when I left about 1923. I lived in and was well looked after. I used to have a half day a week from 3 p.m. until 7 p.m. Later I asked whether this might be extended to 9 p.m. Before this was agreed, Mrs. Ryland cycled down to Henley to see my parents and find out whether they were agreeable to this extension, which they did. Once a month I had a day off. Sometimes I would go into Stratford and on occasions I would visit Birmingham. I was very happy during my stay with Mrs. Ryland. My uniform consisted of a long black dress with stock collar, white starched embroidered apron with wide bow at back and a spotted muslin cap with my hair in a huge bun at the back. When I looked at myself in the mirror for the first time I did not know whether to laugh or cry, but Mrs. Ryland and our cook seemed to think the outfit suited me, so I was pacified.

In fact I began to think I was someone important. All the cooking was done on a huge kitchen range with ovens either side. A steel plate rack which shone like silver from much cleaning above a steel fender wide enough to sit on, which was especially cosy during the winter months. Hot water for baths which we would take to the various rooms in very large cans. Washing up water all came from a copper in the back kitchen. All lighting was by oil lamps and candles.

The family consisted of Mr. & Mrs. Ryland and Mrs. Rylands' mother a Mrs.Onslow, a most gracious lady who was a friend to all in the village. Her bedroom walls were covered with photos and souvenirs connected with her life. There was a very large photograph of her son, who was killed in France in 1916. Underneath this photograph on the mantlepiece was always a small posy of flowers. Every year she would hold a sale of work in aid of a charity, I cannot remember which but for this she worked the whole year making grey flannel petticoats and chemises, aprons and men's shirts, pinafores, socks, stockings, gloves. She would hold a sewing class most weeks when most of the women from the village would attend and help her with items for the sale of work. If anyone was ill or had fallen on hard times Mrs. Onslow was always there ready to help.

We used to rise at 6.30 a.m. and our first job was to light the fire in the kitchen range so as to boil the water for the early morning cup of tea. Prayers were always said before breakfast.

After about two years my sister joined the staff taking on my job whilst I assisted with the cooking. My sister never had another job and married a member of the staff. She still lives in Preston Bagot.

All furniture was polished with bees wax and turps. We would melt the wax by holding it against a warm flat iron and let it drip into a stone jar, then we would add turps and stir.

Spring cleaning was a real chore, every piece of furniture had to be moved from each room. Curtains, bed-clothes, carpets all had to be cleaned. Mats were given a thorough beating and floor boards scrubbed with soft soap.

On one of these occasions my mother and a friend came to help and I thought it would be nice if I laid a tea for them. I boiled an egg each but just as we were about to start Mrs. Ryland came into the kitchen. I was so confused I picked up the eggs and almost threw them into my mother's hat which was still on the side-board. Of course Mrs. Ryland could not help but see what I did. When she saw me the next day she was rather annoyed because she thought it had been very thoughtful of me to provide for my mother and friend after the work they had done.

As we girls got older some would become engaged then there was plenty of activity with knitting cushions, crochet work and anything you could afford to buy for your new home would go in what we called the "bottom draw" until such time as the girl was married.

After some six years at Preston Bagot House I decided to leave. With two friends, one was a Miss Yarwood, we obtained jobs at Lapworth Rectory. At this time my fiancee, now my husband, decided to join the Army and this seemed to unsettle me. I was sorry to leave Mrs. Ryland, it would not have taken much to persuade me to stay, but I had also become tired of cooking and decided to return to front of house work as a parlour maid.

Being at the Rectory was more like working in a hotel, there seemed to be so many visitors. The Rev and Mrs. Bell and their three sons lived at the Rectory. There were three maids. There was a cow kept for supplying milk. The churning of milk was done in a cellar. There was no gas or electricity. Hip baths were placed in each bedroom at night together with a can of cold water. Hot water was taken up each morning. The water was always in the bath the next morning so I assume they always took their bath.

One of the sons of the house was very keen on wireless and he had left a pair of earphones on the window sill. Filled with curiosity I put them to my ear and was startled out of my life to hear a voice announcing 2.LO 2.LO. I thought someone must have been standing behind me and was quite relieved when I turned round to find that I was quite alone.

I was only at the Rectory for a year or so when the staff were reduced because of the sons had either gone abroad or into business in London. I next took a job in Dorridge as a cook. This house had all mod cons. Compared with what I had been used to. We had hot and cold water laid on which was a real treat. Electricity, even a carpet sweeper. Things were beginning to change, this was about the middle twenties. Our dress for instance had shorter skirts, smart matinee aprons, straight caps with velvet ribbon threaded through and tied at the back. The colour of our dress changed from black to grey with turned down collars. Whilst I was working here the mistress of the house asked me if I would help her sister who lived in a large house at Clent, this was only for a short period. The experience was the high light of my life up till then. The parties they gave were wonderful. I was required to go into Stourbridge to collect flowers and fruit. They entertained many society guests and I remember we had a party of Hungarians to entertain on one occasion. The Butler was a Mr. Dammant, he was always referred to as 'Dam it' — out of his hearing of course. I was only at Clent for about six weeks before I was required to return to my employer at Dorridge. I was really sorry to have to leave Clent.

I had to leave my job at Dorridge after about two years because my father became seriously ill and my mother, being deaf, found it difficult to manage. My father finally died after an illness lasting almost two years, that was in 1928. I felt I ought to obtain a job locally so that I could assist at home. I managed to secure a position with Canon and Mrs. Cartwright at the Rectory which was where Barclays Bank now stands. I commenced as a cook and during my stay I must have made gallons of Beef Tea and Baked Custard which was given to the sick and needy. It was a happy household. The Rector and his wife were constantly answering the door either to visitors or people in need who were never turned away.

It was in August 1930 that Canon Cartwright was taken ill and died very suddenly. He died actually on the day I was to be 'asked in Church' for the first time. Today we call it reading 'the banns'.

I was married from 191 High Street. Prior to our wedding my husband, who was a regular soldier, had been in India for six years. During this time I never missed writing to him once a week.

One of my wedding presents was a pillow given to us by Mrs. Michael Bell (Widow of Keble Howard, writer and son of one of the Rectors of Henley). This pillow was stuffed with chicken feathers and was made by a Mrs. Harris who lived in a cottage opposite to the Red Lion. She dressed poultry for all sorts of people, Arden House School and Glendossal.

In view of Canon Cartwrights death a Mr. Miller, a relief Curate from Stepney East London, married us at St. Johns. I had been secretary of the G.F.S. for some fourteen years and members formed a choir at my wedding. Mrs. Agar played the organ. There was no honeymoon.

Our first home was at 249 High Street where both my son and daughter were born. We were there for about five years before moving to our present address in Cherry Orchard, No. 18. We considered ourselves very fortunate to get this council owned house. I think there must have been a good hundred children amongst the families living on this estate, but they were never any trouble.

My husband's first job was with a Mr. S. Newcombe who owned the gravel pits at Kington. My husband worked for Mr. Newcombe until the outbreak of the second World War when he was called up because he was still on the Army Reserve. In a way it was a blessing in that my husband had to stop work at the gravel pits. His work was outside and in all weathers and as a result of the damp conditions he had developed some rhumatism. He was earning 10d per hour whilst working, no pay when the weather was too bad to work. There was no pay even for Bank Holidays. I can remember that my week-end joint did not have to exceed 3/-. I used to have two cwt of coal (4/-) which I used to try and buy every week of the year. Tradesmen would call, such as the butcher and the baker, even for the smallest order. Mrs. Hewins was our milk lady who had a little three wheel cart with a big churn in it. She also sold rabbits at a 1/- each. I have been to the market which was held at the back of the White Swan and bought a dozen chicks for a 1/- and reared them under a mop-head suspended from a chair. I remember once bidding for a goose at the market just before Christmas. It was knocked down to me for 6/-. A man then advised me to put it back in the auction, he said I could make myself a bob or two, so I put this Goose back in an empty case at the end of the row and it was sold for 8/- so I made a couple of shillings over that deal.

Normally we would kill one of the cockerels we had reared, for our christmas dinner. Although it was difficult to manage on the money my husband earned we always looked forward to Christmas.

Round about harvest time my husband and I would go off on our bikes, 'leasing', gathering up the odd bits of corn we found in the fields, this was to feed our fowl. We thoroughly enjoyed this little venture. I used to love to hear the cockerels crowing, nearly everyone had fowl so you can imagine each of these cocks calling one another. It is one of the sounds I miss today.

Most people grew vegetables and we would swop with one another. Another outing I enjoyed was to go 'Wooding' on our bikes, picking up dead branches and pieces of wood which helped to save coal.

In our new home in Cherry Orchard whilst we had a bath it had no waste, so you had to fill it and empty it with a bucket. We obtained our hot water from the copper which had a fire underneath. A Mr. Woodhall brought paraffin round to the houses in a horse drawn cart. He lived in one of the cottages just beyond Edge Lane on the Warwick Road. The name of the cottage was Beggars Bush.

I joined the W.I. in 1931 but could not attend every meeting because of my young family.

A person who stands out in my memory for her kindness was May Foden. She was a Sunday School teacher at the Baptist Church. She would visit anyone who was unwell. Unfortunately she was not very old when she died.

Looking back over my life, I have been married 48 years and really most everything has turned out alright. I am glad I lived when I did, everyone was so happy, we seemed to share one anothers troubles, a sense of service, but there seems nothing like that today. People always seem to want to be paid for anything they do today, we never expected any such thing. I say to myself on occasions a little prayer that I came across:-

"God give me the serenity to accept the things I cannot change
Courage to change the things I can and wisdom to know the difference"
It's the wisdom to know the difference that I am lacking in.
It's wonderful to look back on such a happy life.

My husband I are looking forward to celebrating our Golden Wedding in 1980.

Mr Townsend died in 1984. Mrs. Townsend died in 1987.

Enid Doreen Trinder (nee Hadley)

I was born on the 19th February, 1914 at No. 78 High Street but we were there for only a few weeks after I was born, before moving to No. 28 High Street. I had two sisters but there was a gap of eight or nine years between us. My father was born in Henley but my mother came from Lapworth. Our cottage consisted of a living room and an area which served as kitchen, scullery — it was very small. Upstairs there was one bedroom and a tiny box room. Under the stairs was a small area which served as a pantry. We did have a water tap which was outside and during the winter months would often freeze up; to thaw it out we would set light to newspapers placed under the tap.

I went, as most children, to the school on the High Street close to the ice-ceam parlour. I cannot say that I excelled at any particular subject. I enjoyed sewing and needlework. Our classes were mixed, about 30 children to a class. I think there were about seven classes in the school. When we became older we were marched along the High Street to what is now Brook House (47 High Street) where we were taught cookery. If you took your own ingredients you were allowed to bring home whatever you had made and cooked. If you could afford it you were able to buy other things that had been made. Towards the end of our schooling the girls were instructed in laundering, the boys used the same building but for wood-work. On Sunday the building was used for the Church of England Sunday School.

I left school in April 1928 and was given a school leaving certificate which I still have. On it is printed 'You should take care of this card, it will help you obtain employment'. It also gives a character reference.

My earliest memories of Christmas were the very big fires we had and there was also nuts and fruit on the table which were not there at other times. To help save the coal my father would mix the coal dust with potato peelings and tea leaves. Those people who kept a pig would have kept these to mix in with the food but my parents never did keep a pig. I was fairly fortunate compared with some children at Christmas time because I would most likely receive a doll or a book or building bricks. I was in effect an only child for the first eight years of my life. I had an aunt living at Lapworth who always gave me a present at Christmas time. Speaking of this aunt my father would often put me in a pram and wheel me to see her; that must have been a round trip of 10/12 miles.

I think I am right in saying that for Christmas dinner we had roast beef and of course Christmas pudding. A cutting from a holly bush would serve as our Christmas tree. I remember being thrilled one christmas when my father brought home an old car battery which he wired to a lamp bulb, which was hung amongst the holly. When it was switched on, it really was an occasion.

My father drove the first bus in Henley for Bob Newcombe. That was about 1926.

RECORD OF EMPLOYMENT.

Nature of Employment.	Date of Beginning	Ending	Signature of employer

Changes of Address (to be entered by holder)

SCHOOL LEAVING CARD.

This card issued on behalf of the Warwickshire Education Committee, to

(Full name of Pupil) *Enid Doreen Hadley*

of

Address *28 High St.*

Henley in Arden

(Signed) *R. Khatki* Head Teacher. Date. *11/11/1928*

If you take this card to

(Head Teacher................................
and place of nearest Evening School, if any).................................

it will admit you free of charge to the Preparatory or First Year's Course.

You are recommended to take the greatest care of this card, as it may be the means of helping you to obtain work in after life.

4000 v 21 303.

School leaving Card.

I cannot be sure when it started but my father would give me a penny each Saturday which I would usually spend on sweets at Betsy Smith's who had a small sweet shop to the left of what was the Tan Yard (85/89 High Street). Sometimes I would go to Sally Argyle's parents shop, she was one of our school teachers, the shop was next to the White swan and sold newspapers and stationery.

Another treat, it was always a case of if you had the money, was to visit Mrs. Satchwell House, which was where Marjorie Hope has her shop (99 High Street). On Fridays only she would cook faggots and peas. Something like this was really a treat after the plain food we had most days.

There was also a Mr. Cheshire who had a pork butchers shop next to where Barclays Bank is, he would also cook faggots and peas but I cannot be certain whether that was on Fridays only.

One of my sisters had scarlet fever and was taken to the Isolation Hospital at Stratford. I can't remember how many times my mother took me to see her but we would walk there and back. We used to talk to my sister through an open window.

It must have been in the late twenties when we had a motor fire engine; whenever there was a fire someone would run up the street ringing a bell to summon the firemen. There were occasions when the motor would not start and required a push, I've known it to be towed to get it started.

DOREEN HADLEY

SCHOOL RECORD.

Date of Birth...*19/2/14*............   Name of School.*Henley in Arden C*

Entered School on......*3/4/*............192*2*   Left on .....*5/4/*............192*8*

Age on leaving..........*14*......years.....*1*......months.

General report as to character, work, conduct, and special aptitude (if any).

Good in every respec/

Signed........*A H Walke*........Head {Master / ~~Mistress~~}   Date......*4/4/*............192*8*

SECONDARY, EVENING, OR TECHNICAL SCHOOL.

Year and Month of Entering Leaving	Name and Type of School.	Subject.*	Attendance‡	Merit and Progress of Work.‡	Signature of Teacher.

To be filled in for Evening and Technical Schools only.
‡ V.G.=Very Good.   G.=Good.   V.F.=Very Fair.   F.=Fair.   P.=Poor.   B=Bad.

School Record.

On New Year's Eve hand bell ringers would go up and down the street ringing in the New Year.

All our policemen were friendly and would speak to you but they were very strict, if you did something wrong you knew all about it. We had a

Walter Hadley was Mrs. Trinder's Father.

P.C. Ducmanton. I remember him, he was so smart with his moustache trimmed and waxed.

We always looked forward to Bank Holidays. Whit Monday was carnival day, there would be bands from local towns. On the August Tuesday we had the flower show which was held in the field opposite to the present Sports & Social Club.

We were married in 1936.

Mr. William Trinder

I was born on the 2nd June, 1906 near to Crabbs Cross which is near Redditch. I had six brothers and sisters. My father was unable to find permanent employment and we were constantly on the move from farm to farm in the counties of Warwickshire and Staffordshire. My father claimed to have lived in 42 different cottages during his working life, most of them were tied houses. This moving around meant that I was never at any one school for any length of time. I once attended the Catholic school at Wootton Wawen for a short period. On one occasion we lived in the Toll Cottage at the top of Henley High Street, it was in very poor condition. We spent two spells at the Tan Yard in Henley which was situated between 85/ 87 High Street. There were six or seven cottages and one bungalow built

An early vehicle belonging to a member of the Newcombe family.

down the left hand side of what was a large court yard; you entered under an archway from the street, there were two wooden gates but these were never closed, I suppose they would have been in use when the property was used as a tanning factory. There was no water laid on to any of the cottages, you drew your water from two taps, one at either end of the row of cottages. There was a communal wash house at the bottom of the yard which was referred to as the brew house; the women had to arrange among themselves what day they did their washing. Gas was laid on but I suppose it was due to the poor pressure that the light given was little better than a candle.

There were no back doors to any of these cottages, you entered the front door and stepped down one step into the living room. In the corner of this room were stairs which led up to a single bedroom and a very small box room. Under the stairs was our pantry. Behind the living room was a small area which served as a kitchen. There were three of four privies which were shared by everyone, these were situated just before you came to the row of cottages, they were not the flush type just big buckets which were collected by a man with his horse and dray cart. I can't remember how often he would call. Looking back on the inhabitants of those cottages, somehow they all appear to have been characters in one way or another. There can be no denying we were very poor, we never had more than one and a half slices of bread at any meal. If we should have eggs two of us would share a single egg, finish with half a cup of tea. You could get a penny worth of stale cakes

P.C. Challis who served with P.C. Ducmanton.

from Welch's bakery, these were better than the so called fresh cakes of today. Quite often I would be sent down to the Yew Trees where I would wait on the opposite side of the road. The people who lived there would know what I was waiting for and they would send out bread and sometimes cakes. They were very kind.

There was one time when we lived in a cottage close by the osier beds in Pettiford Lane, my Dad and I worked there for a time stripping canes. Whenever we wanted coal I used to take a small trolley and go to the old station yard at the top of Henley High Street and fetch ½ cwt. That must be a trip of about four miles and of course the sun wasn't always shining.

I left school, in 1920 but like my father I found work hard to come by. I can remember one farm I worked on, where I was living in, we had boiled bacon one morning for breakfast which was infested with maggots so I slipped it inside my shirt until I got outside, then disposed of it. Of course there was no fridges in those days. In the end I joined the army in 1928 and did seven years. In 1936 we were married but in 1939 I was called up because I was still on the reserve.

Henley-in-Arden Court Leet

Local government originally was invested in the Court Leet and Court Baron (Lord of the Manor). The Court Baron was mainly concerned with land law, inheritance and the more serious crimes, while the Court Leet was concerned with law & order, nuisances, fair trading and the like.

The Court Leet and Court Baron of the Manor of Henley-in-Arden is one of the few Manorial Courts which have survived, although today it serves purely as a focus for civic dignity without any power other than that of suggestion. In 1976, under a new statute passed by Parliament, this Court is exempt from the act which abolishes extinct and antiquaited Courts. The High Bailiff still takes the lead in most public matters in the town; his chain of office was presented by Mr. W. J. Fieldhouse, C.B.E. J.P. (Lord of the Manor 1914 – 1928) in 1919 to commemorate the signing of the peace treaty following the first World War. A very close relationship exists with other Courts at Alcester, Bromsgrove and Warwick.

Meetings of the Court are still held in the upper storey of the Guildhall which is a 15th Century timber framed building. The roof timbers are thought to have come from dismantled ships at Bristol then floated up river. Another view is that they might have come from the derelict Beaudesert Castle. The window frames, doors and fireplace form part of the renovations paid for by Mr. W. J. Fieldhouse, round about 1915. The ground floor is at present rented to the Warwickshire County Council and serves the town as a library.

Court Leet Elections are still held annually on the second Wednesday in November. Election of officers is by Jurors who are towns people with a residential qualification of five years. The public are welcomed to attend these meetings, which are held in the evening, commencing 7.30 p.m. The opening and closing ceremony is performed by the Town Crier, who is a member of the Court. All officers are robed and wear badges denoting their office in exactly the same way as their predecessors did when holding official office.

Officers of the Henley Court Are:-
Steward, High Bailiff, Low Bailiff, Constable, Mace Bearer, Butter Weigher, Ale Taster, Brook Lookers, 2, Affearors, 2. Town Crier. There is also a Chaplain to the Court who is usually the Parish Priest.

Their duties in the past were:-

The Steward.
Would have presided over all meetings in the absence of the Lord of the

Manor and have been responsible for the recordings of all matters that came before the Court.

The High Bailiff.
Responsible for all laws and maintenance of good order and the upholding of justice without fear or favour, with the aid of his officers in the name of the Lord of the Manor.

Mace Bearer & Constable.
Would precede the High Bailiff at official meetings and functions. Signs of Authority and Law.

Affearors.
Would assess and confirm fines imposed by the Court on persons who were in breach of the peace or had offended against the law.

Butter Weigher Ale Taster.
Each was to ensure that correct weights and measures were maintained and prices agreed were kept.

Brook Lookers.
Responsible for ensuring that the River Alne and its tributaries were kept free from refuse.

Town Crier.
To call all public notices.

It would appear from the Court Rolls that Courts were held twice a year. These are some of the cases taken from the Court records.

13th October, 1593.
We order that all the Ale Howse Kepers and Victelers within the liberties shall make good and holsome ale and beare for mans bodie and that they and every one of them sell the same for two pence half-penny a gallon new and three pence stale and everyone denying to sell as aforesaide shall forfett for every offence XIId.

20th October, 1619.
Under the list of 'Paines and orders' warning that no one shall abuse Mr. Baylife in calling him knave or giving him any other unmanerly words. The fine for so doing being 40/-.

20th October, 1620.
Eleanor Powell was presented for that she is a scold (rude glamorous woman, modern definition) and lives unquietly. Judgement that she shall be

cucked in the cocking-stool (these duckings would take place in the brook the woman being exposed to the scorn and derision of the on-lookers).

24th October. 1656.
Ric. Reeve, Tho. Stocke and John Stocke are common butchers and have eache of them since the last Court killed one calfe under five weeks ould against the forme of the statute etc. Therefore every of them hath forfetted the somme of 6/- but by the favour of the Court the same is moderated to XIId. peece.

4th November, 1799.
Josiah Bott having been appointed High Bailiff for the year ensuing and having had a weeks notice to attend this Court to be sworn and having been also applied to this day to come to the Court and be sworn into his office and the said Josiah Bott having neglected so to do is fined by the Court in the sum of five pounds.

25th October, 1819.
This Court under the chairmanship of Thomas Hunt, Gentleman, Steward of the Manor.

There were 31 persons presented for being responsible for putting up a Bow Window in some cases two Bow Windows on the Lords waste (an infringement of the recognised building line) 7 others were presented for enclosing the Lords Waste in various places. There is no record of any fines being imposed but there is a statement that the Affearors having examined the fines and penalties before set and affixed do approve and allow for the same.

Ordered that this Court stand adjourned and the same is hereby adjourned to the first Monday of May next to be then holden at the Swann Inn in Henley-in-Arden within this Manor.

Although the records of High Bailiff only go back to 1477 it is certain that Court Leets operated much earlier. It is recorded that in the 13th century it was customary in the early morning of the day on which a market or fair was to take place, for the High Bailiff and all his officers to parade the town and warn all rogues, vagabonds, cutpurses and idly and disorderly persons to depart or remain at their peril. No doubt possible law breakers could be overawed by the majesty and dignity of the towns rulers and perhaps not unmindful of the various punishments which they had the power to impose would decide in most cases to leave town.

In 1449 King Henry VI granted a charter to the Lord of the Manor of Henley-in-Arden, at that time Sir Ralph Boteler, confirming all the rights and privileges that had gone before and were to continue in the future. This Charter with its Seal hangs in the Guildhall.

Guildhall first floor. Court Leet elections and other court meeting are held here.

Carnival Queen escorted by High Bailiff John Whitehouse (1965-1968) proceeded by Court Constable — H. Perkins followed by other members of the court — Phillip Garston-Jones (member of T.V. serial the Archers). Michael Hawkes (Butcher), Ron Boroughs (Manager Lloyds Bank).

Lords of the Manor of Henley-in-Arden

Lord of the Manor before the conquest was one Wagene (or Waga as he is called in Domesday) Wootton signifies the 'Town in the Wood'.

The Conqueror stripped Wagene of his possessions and granted them to Robert De Tonie otherwise 'de Stafford' who in turn granted them to Thurston de Montford, Kinsman of Henry of Newburgh, first Earl of Warwick.

1066	Wagene.
1086	Robert de Stafford
	Stephen Thurstan de Montfort
	Henry II, Henry de Montfort
	Henry II. Thurstan de Montfort II
1216	Peter de Montfort
1265	Thomas de Clare
1267	Peter de Montfort II
1287	John de Montfort
1296	John de Montfort II
1313	Peter de Montfort
1326	John de Lobbenham
1369	Thomas de Beauchamp
	Earl of Warwick
1376	Sir William de Beauchamp
1385	Sir Baldwin Freville &
	Sit Thomas Boteler
1441	Sir Ralph Boteler
1474	Sir John Norbury &
	Henry Belknap
1478	Edward IV
1483	Edward V
1483	Richard III
1485	Henry VII
1509	Henry VIII
1547	Edward VI
1547	John Dudley, Earl of Warwick
1553	Queen Mary
1562	Ambrose Dudley, Earl of Warwick
1589	Queen Elizabeth
1591	William Harman
1592	Thomas Spencer
1610	Anne, Queen of James I

1614	William White
1637	William Baldwyn
1649	Commonwealth
1656	Richard Walker
1673	Thomas Archer
1685	Andrew Archer
1742	Sir Thomas. 1st Baron Archer of Umberslade
1768	Sir Andrew 2nd Baron Archer of Umberslade
1790	The Right Hon the Earl of Plymouth. Christopher Musgrave Esq., Henry Howard Esq., Edward Bolton Clive Esq.,
1801	The Right Hon. William Pitt, Lord Amherst, Sarah, Lady Amherst (late Countess of Plymouth) Christopher Musgrave Esq., Henry Howard Esq., Edward Bolton Clive Esq
1812	Christopher Musgrave Esq.,
1840	The Hon. Anne Elizabeth Musgrave.
1850	Captain Christopher Musgrave
1873	Darwin Galton Esq.,
1903	Mrs. P. E. Galton
1912	Edward Galton Wheler Esq.,
1914	William John Fieldhouse Esq., C.B.E. J.P.
1928	Olive Nancy Bernard
1957	Olive Nancy Bernard
1974	Timothy Huntley Robinson
1990	Joseph Alex. Hardy

Honarary Burgesses

1919   Charles Couchman.
1923   William Ernest Nelson. O.B.E.
1946   Willoughby Agar. J.P.
1949   Harry Hawkes.
1957   John Foster Drake. D.F.C. B.E.M.
1960   Rupert Oates Nevitt.
1975   Frederick Stuart Lodder. T.D.
1978   William Neville Hawkes.
1983   Harry Norman Welch.

Persons who have rendered special services to the Community of Henley-in-Arden.

With the exception of John Drake all were former High Bailiffs of Henley-in-Arden,

High Bailiffs of Henley-in-Arden

1477	John Rufford		1674/5	John Hemynge
1482	William Pye		1675/6	William Horsley
1485	Edward Brierton		1677/8	William Jones
	(or Brereton)		1694/5	Thomas Williams
1518	Edmund Brierton		1722/3	Thomas Baker
1537	John Holmes		1723/4	John Maynard
1569	William Smith		1724/5	John Morrel
1592	Thomas Whelere		1725/6	Thomas Haines
1592/3	John Baker		1726/7	William Yates
1593/4	Robert Wheatley		1727/8	Robert Morrel
1595/6	William Whateley		1728/9	John Savage
1596/7	John Bellars		1729/30	William Horsley
1567/8	Christopher Holmes		1730/31	William Williams
1598/9	Richard Holmes		1731/2	John Ward
1599/1	Nicholas Watton		1732/3	John Steward
1601/2	Daniel Heminges		1733/4	Edward Sale
1602/3	William Whatley		1734/5	Daniel White
1605/6	John Hemminges		1735/6	Thomas Ballard
1606/7	William Chambers		1736/7	Samuel Baker
1607/8	Thomas Cowper		1737/8	William Cowper
1608/9	Richard Holmes		1738/9	Thomas Williams
1609/10	Symon Bellers		1739/40	John Caddick
1610/11	Nicholas Watton		1740/1	Joseph Haynes
1612/13	Francis Sly		1741/2	John Haynes
1613/14	William Kerby, Baker		1742/3	Samuel Ward
1614/15	William Chambers		1743/4	Robert Pettit
1615/16	William Smyth		1744/5	John Lea
1616/17	Richard Key		1745/6	William Savage
1617/18	John Heming, snr.		1746/7	John Steward
1618/19	Thomas Cowper		1747/8	Thomas Round
1619/20	John Baker		1748/9	Francis Charles
1620/21	Richard Jeninges		1749/50	George Bell
1622/23	John Jones		1750/1	John Chamberlain
1624/25	Nicholas Watton		1752/3	John Maynard
1627/8	William Chambers		1753/4	Thomas Knowles
1628/9	William Smyth		1754/5	Benjamin Horsley
1629/30	John Holmes		1755/6	John London
1635/6	William Bailis		1756/7	William Mander
1637/38	Richard Knight		1757/8	Hopkins Horsley

1638/39	Robert Bannester	1758/9	Stephen Shepard
1639/40	William Cowper	1759/62	John Hoitt
1640/41	William Chambers	1762/3	William Biddle
1641/42	John Holmes	1763/4	Richard London
1642/43	John Whately	1764/5	James Baker
1643/4	Richard Reeve	1765/6	James Ward
1647/8	Richard Whatley	1766/7	William Birch
1656/7	Francis Baker	1767/8	Thomas Ward
1673/4	Thomas Cowper	1768/9	Thomas Tibbatts
1769/70	John Harborne	1910/22	Dr. William Ernest Nelson
1770/1	William Chambers	1922/26	William Thomas Taylor J.P.
1771/2	James Horsley	1926/30	Harry Hawkes
1772/3	Francis Alexander	1930/45	Willoughby Agar
1773/4	John Eaves	1945/48	John Pemberton Nelson
1774/5	Joseph Taylor	1948/50	Harry Norman Welch
1775/6	Benjamin Haynes	1950/53	Frederick Stuart Lodder
1776/7	John Clarke	1953/57	Rupert Oates Nevitt
1777/8	Thomas Burman	1957/58	John Pemberton Nelson
1778/9	William Izod	1958/61	William Neville Hawkes
1779/80	Richard Tibbatts	1961/64	Kenneth Howard Terry
1780/1	William Parkes	1964/65	Charles Henry Slingsby
1781/2	John Green	1965/68	John Maxwell Whitehouse
1782/5	John Haynes	1968/71	Derek Keith Sharman
1785/92	John Kemp	1971/74	Harold Eric Bloomer
1792/99	Isaac Court	1974/76	Alan Lewis Butler
1799/1801	Joseph Bott	1976/79	Walter Henry Collins
1801/19	William James	1979/81	Edward J. Nicholson
1819/40	Thomas J. P. Burman	1981/83	Bernard Edward O'Donnell
1840/5	Thomas Wowen Jones	1983/84	Brian Jackson
1845/50	Dr. Hugh Francis Burman	1984/86	John Latham
1850/55	William Batchelor Dimmond	1986/88	Robert Charles Welham
1855/73	Thomas Barnes Couchman	1988/90	Keith Alan Ford
1873/93	John Hannett	1990/92	Duncan Bainbridge
1893/1910	Charles Couchman	1993	Alec S. Halliwell

"LIFE FROM THE PAST"

INVOICE 786

P. T. Beck & B. J. Wilkins
RADIO, TELEVISION, SALES AND SERVICES,
ELECTRICAL INSTALLATIONS.

199, HIGH STREET, HENLEY-IN-ARDEN,
WARWICKSHIRE.

HENLEY GARAGES LTD.
HIGH STREET,
HENLEY-IN-ARDEN
Telephone : HENLEY 43

CHARGE TO .... SIGNED ....

CREDIT	PETROL	CASH

M r. .... School Hill, Woeton, ... 25th. May 19 55

21st. April 55
Repairs to M/R. Iron.

1	Green M/R. lamp		9½
1	M/R. Handle	6	-
1	M/R. heat control knob	1	3
	Electricians ti : removing old & fitting above new parts	3	6
		11	6½

002526 CUSTOMER'S SIGNATURE

To be produced on demand—NOT TRANSFERABLE (See Condition 7 Overleaf)   ISSUE FEE £3

WIRELESS TELEGRAPHY ACT, 1949   **BROADCAST RECEIVING LICENCE (Including Television)**   General Form   PLUS DUTY £1

This Licence expires on the last day of ..... OCT ..... TB 497740

035761

HENLEY-IN-ARDEN AND BEAUDESERT

JUBILEE CELEBRATIONS

MONDAY, MAY 6th, 1935.

PROGRAMME.

PROGRAMME.

10 - 0 a.m. Children's Service at Baptist Church.

11-15 a.m. A procession will be formed at the Market Cross, headed by the High Bailiff: (W. Agar, Esq.), and Court Leet and the various public bodies of the township, and proceed to St. John's Church for an United Thanksgiving Service.

2-30 p.m. A programme of Sports has been arranged comprising foot races for all ages, Slow cycle races for boys and girls, Sack and obstacle races, 3 legged races, Tug-o'War, Bowling for a pig. Bumping Match, etc., to take place on the Cricket Field, (by kind permission of C. R. Parsons, Esq.), and continue until 6-30. *Presentation of prizes will take place immediately after each event.*
A Bowling Competition will be held on the "White Swan" Green, from 2-30 onwards. Bowls will be provided and prizes given by the "White Swan" Bowling Club.

4-30 p.m. Children's Tea and presentation of Jubilee Mugs, etc., at Messrs. Welch's Pavilion, free to all Henley children from 3 to 14 years of age, with tickets, obtainable from Mr. Pearse or Mrs. Hawes.

6-30 p.m. Old People's Supper at the Church of England Schools, to ticket holders.

6-30 p.m. Maypole Dancing by the younger children to be followed by general dancing in Fancy Dress at Market Place, for which prizes will be given.

8 - 0 p.m. Broadcast of the King's Speech to the Nation (at Market Cross).

8-30 p.m. Maypole Dancing for older children to be followed by general dancing.

9-30 p.m. A Torchlight procession will be formed and proceed to Beaudesert Mount, (by kind permission of F. Hopkins, Esq.), where a Bonfire will be lighted under the direction of Mr. F. S. Lodder, and the Henley Rat Club.

10 - 0 p.m. Signal maroon, and lighting of Bonfire by Mrs. Willoughby Agar. Rockets will be fired at intervals.

Dancing in the Market Square will continue until midnight.

Judging for the best decorated business premises, private houses and Cottages will take place during the day, and the prizes for this event will be awarded after the King's broadcast.

(Warning : Do not get too close to Bonfire.)

Teas and refreshments may be obtained during the afternoon at Messrs. Welch's Pavilion, at reasonable charges.

Music and Announcements throughout the proceedings by FEWTRELL'S SUPER SOUND SYSTEM.

"GOD SAVE THE KING AND QUEEN."

There will be flood-lighting of St. John's Church Tower from North and South sides; of the Guild Hall, and of the Street in the vicinity of the Market Cross, by Mr. A. Fewtrell.

Teas will be available from 3-30 p.m. onwards, at Messrs. Welch's Pavilion, at a charge of 1/- each.

Licensed Bar at the Pavilion (by Mr. Swainston, of the Blue Bell Hotel), from 2 p.m. to 6 p.m.

"GOD SAVE THE KING AND QUEEN."

General Committee:

Chairman : Dr. W. Agar, High Bailiff.
Vice-Chairman : Mr. R. L. Newcombe, Low Bailiff.

Hon. Secretary : Mr. S. Wakefield.
Hon. Treasurer : Mr. J. F. Drake.

Finance Committee : Members of the Court Leet :-

Constable, Mr. Harry Hodges; Ale Taster, Mr. A. R Hawkes; Butter Weigher, Mr. George Coppage; Brook Lookers, Mr. Norman Welch and Mr. A. Bayliss; Mace Bearer, Mr. O. James; Affearors, Mr. W. E. Hemming and Mr. J. L. Mason; Town Crier, Mr. N. B. Harris.

Chaplain to the High Bailiff, Rev. W. J. Easterbrook, (Rector of Henley-in-Arden and Beaudesert).

Chairmen of Sub-Committees:

Catering, Mrs. Newcombe; Children's, Mrs. Easterbrook; Sports, Captain Nevitt; Carnival, Major Slingsby; Bonfire, Mr. John Lodder; Decorations, Sergeant Newell; Illuminations, Mr A. Fewtrell.

STEPHENS, Henley-in-Arden.

HENLEY-IN-ARDEN AND BEAUDESERT

CORONATION CELEBRATION

WEDNESDAY, MAY 12th, 1937.

PROGRAMME.

PROGRAMME

Sunday, May 9th.

11 - 0 a.m. Court Leet and members of other Public Bodies to assemble at the Market Cross, and proceed in procession to St. John's Church to attend Service of Prayer and Thanksgiving at 11-15.

Wednesday, May 12th. (CORONATION DAY)

Peals on Bells of St. John's Church, early morning and at intervals during the day.

8 - 0 a.m. Holy Communion at St. Nicholas Church.

9 - 0 a.m. Children's Service at St. John's Church.

10 - 0 a.m. Special Service of Intercession at St. John's Church.

1 - 0 p.m. Dinner to residents over 60 years of age of Henley and Beaudesert at the Public Hall.

1-15 p.m. Carnival Procession assembles at the Golden Cross. (South End).

1-30—2 p.m. Judging of Carnival entries. Bushill Matthews, Esq., Festival Organiser,British Drama League, has kindly consented to come and judge the entries.

2 - 0 p.m. Carnival Procession to Sports Ground. (Field kindly lent by C. R. Parsons, Esq).

2-30 p.m. Procession disperses on Sports Ground.

2-45—5 p.m. Sports.
[In consequence of the softness of the Pitch, the proposed Cricket Match, (Victorians v. Rest), has been cancelled].

4-0—6 p.m. A "Running Tea," free to residents of Henley and Beaudesert only, at the Public Hall.

4-30 p.m. Tea at Messrs. Welch's Pavilion free for all Children from 4 to 14 years of age, inclusive, resident in Henley and Beaudesert.

5-30 p.m. Presentation of Coronation Mugs to Children, by Mrs. Willoughby Agar.

6-30 p.m. Dancing by Children and Community Singing in the street near the Market Cross, (arranged by Mrs. Nicholas, Henley-in-Arden Amateur Operatic Society, and Music from the Fewtrell Super Sound System).

7-20—8 p.m. Broadcast at Market Cross of Empire Premiers' Speeches and King George's Gracious Message.

8—9-30 p.m. Street Dancing. M.C. - Mr. Jack Thompson.

9-30 p.m. A Torchlight Procession will be formed at the Market Cross and proceed to the first Beaudesert Hill, (by kind permission of Mrs. Hopkins). An illuminated tableau, representing the Crown, will be formed on the slope of the hill under the direction of Mrs. Nicholas.

10-0 p.m. After the formation of the Tableau, a bonfire on the hill will be lighted by Mrs. Lodder, and a display of Fireworks will follow. Street Dancing will then be resumed.

Judging for the best decorated houses will take place during the day, three prizes being awarded. Mrs. W. E. Nelson will present the prizes, and also the Carnival awards after the King's message.

[See back]